HOW TO

Pull a
Bird
in
Seven
Languages

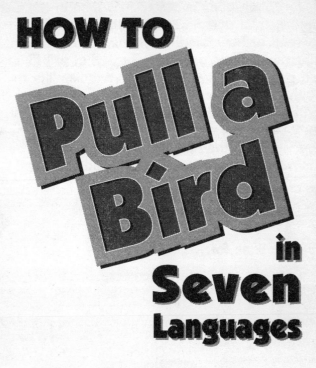

HOW TO Pull a Bird in Seven Languages

The ultimate guide
to success with women
from around the world

CARLTON

You are now holding in your hands one of the most powerful weapons available to a man in the war of the sexes. It doesn't matter where you find yourself or how beautiful the woman you want to impress is; there's a line in here that will fit the bill and get you to first base. Some ladies like to laugh, while others want to be swept off their feet, so the skill in getting the best results from this book lies in correctly reading the girl of your dreams. With the handy translations, you'll be charming in seven languages. Good luck, and remember – a faint heart never won a fair lady!

Contents

Anywhere...

Anywhere...

GB [When you see her waiting for someone] "If he doesn't turn up, I'll be over there."

F [Lorsque vous voyez qu'elle attend quelqu'un] « Si jamais il ne vient pas, je serai juste là-bas. »

D (Wenn sie offensichtlich auf jemanden wartet): „Wenn er nicht kommt komme ich rüber."

I "[Quando noti che lei sta aspettando qualcuno] Se non arriva, sono seduto laggiù."

E "[Las ves esperando a alguien] Si no aparece, me apunto."

P [Enquanto ela espera por alguém] "Se ele não aparecer, estou aqui eu."

S [När du ser henne vänta på någon] "Om han inte dyker upp så sitter jag där borta."

Anywhere...

GB "You could make me very happy with one simple word. May I buy you a drink?"

F « Un simple mot de votre part me rendrait heureux. Puis-je vous offrir un verre ? »

D „ Sie können mich mit einem einzigen Wort sehr glücklich machen. Kann ich Ihnen einen ausgeben ? "

I "Potresti farmi veramente felice con una semplice parola. Posso offrirti da bere?"

E "Me harías muy feliz con una sola palabra. ¿Te puedo invitar a una copa?"

P "Você pode fazer-me muito feliz com uma simples palavra. Posso oferecer-lhe uma bebida?"

S "Du skulle kunna göra mig väldigt lycklig med ett endaste ord. Får jag bjuda på en drink?"

Anywhere...

GB "Do you mind if I stare at you up close instead of from across the room?"

F « Cela ne vous dérange pas si je vous regarde d'un peu plus près plutôt que de vous dévisagez de l'autre bout de la salle/pièce. »

D „ Stört es Sie, wenn ich Sie aus der Nähe anstarre, anstatt vom anderen Ende des Raumes ? "

I "Ti dispiace se ti ammiro da vicino anzichè dall'altro lato della sala?"

E "¿Te importa que te mire desde aquí mismo en lugar de hacerlo desde la otra punta de la sala?"

P "Importa-se que olhe para si de mais perto, em vez de o fazer do outro lado da sala?"

S "Tar du illa upp om jag stirrar på dig härifrån istället för från andra sidan rummet?"

GB "Forgive me, but I'm an artist and it's my job to stare at beautiful women."

F « Pardonnez-moi mais je suis artiste et contemplez les jolies femmes fait partie de mon métier. »

D „Entschuldigung, ich bin Künstler und ich muss einfach schöne Frauen anstarren."

I "Mi perdoni, sono un artista e so che è una deformazione professionale ma non riesco a togliere gli occhi di dosso a una bella donna."

E "Perdona pero soy un artista y tengo que mirar a las mujeres guapas por motivos de trabajo."

P "Desculpe-me mas sou um artista e o meu trabalho é apreciar mulheres lindas."

S "Ursäkta att jag stirrar, men jag är konstnär och det är mitt jobb att betrakta vackra kvinnor."

Anywhere...

GB "Hi, do you want to have my children? OK then, can we just practice?"

F « Bonjour/Bonsoir, cela vous dirait de porter mes enfants ? Bon, d'accord, pourrait-on simplement s'y entraîner alors ? »

D „Hallo, möchten Sie die Mutter meiner Kinder sein ? OK, kein Problem, vielleicht können wir einfach nur üben ? "

I "Ciao, vuoi avere i miei bambini? D'accordo, possiamo allora fare pratica?"

E "Hola ¿quieres ser la madre de mis hijos? Bueno, vale ¿y si sólo praticamos?"

P "Olá, quer filhos comigo? Está bem, nesse caso podemos só praticar?"

S "Hej, vill du ha barn med mig? OK då, men vi kan väl öva?"

Anywhere...

GB "Hi, I make more money than you can spend."

F « Bonjour/Bonsoir, je gagne plus d'argent que vous ne pouvez en dépenser. »

D „Hallo, ich verdiene mehr Geld, als Sie je ausgeben können."

I "Ciao, faccio più soldi di quanti tu riesca a spenderne."

E "Hola, gano más dinero del que puedas gastarte."

P "Olá, eu ganho mais dinheiro, do que o que você consegue gastar."

S "Hej, jag tjänar mer än du kan göra av med."

Anywhere...

GB "I can't decide if you are a better person than you are a woman, or a better woman than you are a person."

F « Je n'arrive pas à me décider. Êtes-vous mieux en tant que personne ou en tant que femme ? »

D „Ich kann mich nicht entscheiden ob Sie interessanter als Person oder als Frau sind."

I "Non riesco a decidermi se sei meglio come persona o come donna, o se sei meglio come donna che come persona."

E "No sabría decir si eres mejor persona que mujer, o mejor mujer que persona."

P "Não consigo decidir se você é melhor pessoa do que mulher, ou se é melhor mulher do que pessoa."

S "Jag kan inte bestämma mig för om du är en bättre person än du är kvinna eller tvärtom."

GB "I have had a really bad day and it always makes me feel better to see a beautiful lady smiling. So, would you smile for me?"

F « J'ai passé une journée vraiment exécrable et une femme souriante me fait toujours du bien. Voudriez-vous me faire un sourire ? »

D „ Ich hatte einen fürchterlichen Tag und es hilft mir immer, wenn ich eine schöne Frau lächeln sehe. Würden Sie bitte für mich lächeln ? "

I "Ho avuto una giornataccia e mi fa sempre sentire meglio vedere una bella donna che sorride. Allora, vorresti farmi un sorriso?"

E "He tenido un día horrible y siempre me alegra ver a una mujer bonita sonriendo. ¿Te importaría sonreírme?"

P "Tive um dia horrível e o que me faz sentir melhor, é ver uma bela mulher a sorrir. Por isso pode sorrir para mim?"

S "Jag har haft en riktigt dålig dag och att se en vacker kvinna le får mig alltid på bättre humör. Så, snälla, du kan väl le?"

Anywhere...

GB "I miss my teddy bear. Will you sleep with me instead?"

F « Mon nounours me manque. Voulez-vous dormir avec moi à sa place ? »

D „ Mein Teddybär fehlt mir. Gehen Sie stattdessen mit mir ins Bett. "

I "Mi manca il mio orsacchiotto. Vuoi dormire con me?"

E "Hecho de menos a mi osito de peluche. ¿Te importa dormir conmigo?"

P "Perdi o meu urso de peluche. Não se importa de dormir comigo para o substituir?"

S "Jag saknar min nallebjörn. Kan inte du sova med mig istället?"

GB "I'd try a cheap chat-up line on you, but you are just too clever."

F « J'essaierais bien une tirade bon marché pour tenter de vous séduire, mais vous êtes bien trop intelligente. »

D „Ich würde eine billig Anmache versuchen, aber Sie sind einfach zu schlau.

I "Potrei usare le classiche frasettine dolci con te, ma tu sei troppo intelligente."

E "Podría intentar ligar contigo con un piropo barato, pero eres demasiado inteligente."

P "Eu estava a tentar uma conversa fiada consigo, mas você é inteligente demais para isso."

S "Jag skulle inte våga mig på en billig raggningsreplik, du är för smart."

Anywhere...

GB "I'm no good at opening lines so why don't we pretend we know each other."

F « Les présentations n'étant pas mon fort, nous pourrions prétendre que nous nous connaissons. »

D „Ich bin nicht besonders gut beim Kennenlernen, können wir vielleicht so tun, als ob wir uns schon kennen? "

I "Non sono tanto bravo a rompere il ghiaccio, perchè allora non facciamo finta che ci conosciamo di già?"

E "No se me dan bien las presentaciones ¿por qué no fingimos que ya nos conocemos?"

P "Não sou muito bom em apresentações, por isso podíamos fingir que já nos conhecemos."

S "Jag är inget bra på kallprat så vi kan väl låtsas att vi känner varandra?"

GB "If your parents hadn't met, I'd be a very unhappy man right now."

F « Si vos parents ne s'étaient pas rencontrés, je serais en ce moment un homme bien malheureux. »

D „Wenn Ihre Eltern sich nicht getroffen hätten, wäre ich jetzt ein sehr unglücklicher Mann. "

I "Se i tuoi genitori non si fossero mai incontrati, a quest'ora sarei stato un uomo veramente infelice."

E "Si tus padres no se hubieran conocido, ahora mismo yo sería un hombre muy desgraciado."

P "Se os seus pais não se tivessem conhecido, eu agora seria um homem muito infeliz."

S "Om dina föräldrar inte hade träffats skulle jag vara en mycket olycklig man just nu."

Anywhere...

GB "In this light, your hair looks like silk."

F « Sous cette lumière, vos cheveux ont l'aspect de la soie. »

D „ In diesem Licht wirkt Ihr Haar wie Seide. "

I "Con questa luce, i tuoi capelli sono come la seta."

E "Con esta luz, tu pelo parece de seda."

P "A esta luz, o seu cabelo parece seda."

S "I det här ljuset ser ditt hår ut som silke."

Anywhere...

GB "It's not true, but I'm going to say "I love you" anyway."

F « Ce n'est pas vrai, mais je vais tout de même le dire "je vous aime". »

D „ Es stimmt zwar nicht, aber ich sage es trotzdem : „„ Ich liebe Sie "". "

I "Non è vero ma voglio lo stesso dirti 'Ti amo'."

E "No es verdad pero de todos modos voy a decirte que 'te quiero'."

P "Não é verdade, mas vou dizer na mesma 'Amo-te'."

S "Det är inte sant, men jag tänker säga 'Jag älskar dig' i alla fall."

Anywhere...

GB "Pardon me, what chat-up line works best on you?"

F « Pardonnez-moi mais quelle est la tirade qui marche pour vous séduire ? »

D „ Entschuldigung, welche Anmache funktioniert am Besten bei Ihnen ? "

I "Mi scusi, ma quale frase di adescamento funziona con lei?"

E Perdona ¿cómo se liga contigo?

P "Perdoe-me mas que tipo de conversa fiada funciona melhor consigo?"

S "Ursäkta mig, hur vill du helst bli uppraggad?"

GB "[Hand her a card reading:] Smile if you'll let me buy you a drink."

F [Tendez-lui une carte qui dit :] « Souriez si vous me laissez vous offrir un verre. »

D (Auf einer Karte, die Sie ihr geben) : „Lächeln Sie bitte, wenn ich Ihnen einen ausgeben kann. "

I [Dalle un biglietto con la scritta] "Sorridi se vuoi che ti offra da bere."

E [Dale una tarjeta que diga:] "Sonríe si dejas que te invite a una copa."

P [Entregando-lhe um cartão] "Sorria se aceita que lhe pague uma bebida."

S [Ge henne ett kort där det står:] "Le, om jag får bjuda på en drink."

Anywhere...

GB "So, what are the chances that we can engage in anything more than just conversation?"

F « Bon, quelles sont les chances de nous engager dans autre chose qu'une conversation ? »

D „ So wie stehen die Chancen, dass wir in mehr als ein interessantes Gespräch verwickelt werden ? "

I "Dimmi che possibilità abbiamo di utilizzare le nostre energie per qualcosa di più che una semplice conversazione?"

E "Así que, ¿qué posibilidades tenemos de enrollarnos en algo más que una conversación?"

P "Então, quais são as hipóteses de nos compromotermos em algo mais do que conversa?"

S "Ska vi inte ägna oss åt något annat än bara konversation?"

GB "Until I saw you, I was certain I was gay. Now I don't know. Please help me find out."

F « Avant de vous voir, j'étais persuadé être homosexuel. Maintenant, je ne sais plus. Aidez-moi à en avoir le cœur net. »

D „Bis ich Sie gesehen habe, war ich sicher, schwul zu sein. Jetzt bin ich nicht mehr so sicher. Bitte helfen Sie mir die Wahrheit rauszufinden. "

I "Prima di vederti, ero sicuro di essere gay. Ma ora non ne sono più così certo. Aiutami a chiarirmi le idee per piacere."

E "Hasta que te he visto estaba seguro de ser gay. Ahora no lo sé. Por favor, ayúdame a descubrirlo."

P "Até a ver, tinha a certeza que era maricas. Agora não sei. Por favor, ajude-se a descobrir."

S "Tills jag såg dig var jag säker på att jag var gay. Nu vet jag inte. Snälla, hjälp mig att ta reda på det."

Anywhere...

GB [Tag behind her as she walks past and ask:] "Where are we going?"

F [Emboîtez-lui le pas alors qu'elle passe devant vous et demandez-lui] « Où allons-nous ? »

D (Gehen Sie ihr nach wenn sie an Ihnen vorbeigeht) : „Wo gehen wir denn hin ? "

I [Seguila quando ti passa vicino e chiedile:] "Dove stiamo andando?"

E [Síguela de cerca cuando pase a tu lado y le preguntas:] "¿A dónde vamos?"

P [Debruçando-se por trás enquanto ela passa] "Onde é que vai?"

S [Häng på när hon går förbi och fråga:] "Vart är vi på väg?"

Anwhere...

GB "What can I do to make you mine?"

F « Que puis-je faire pour que vous soyez mienne ? »

D „Was kann ich tun, um Sie die Meine zu machen ? "

I "Cosa devo fare per farti mia?"

E "¿Qué puedo hacer para que seas mía?"

P "O que posso fazer para que você seja minha?"

S "Vad behöver jag göra för att du skall bli min?"

Anywhere...

GB "You know, I have a romantic side... let's go back to my place and see how long it takes you to find it."

F «Vous savez, j'ai un côté romantique... allons chez moi et voyons combien de temps il vous faut pour le découvrir.»

D „Wissen Sie, ich habe eine romantische Ader... kommen Sie mit zu mir, und finden heraus, wie lange es dauert, sie zu finden."

I "Credimi quando ti dico che c'è un aspetto romantico in me ... vieni a casa mia e vediamo quanto tempo ci impieghi per trovarlo."

E "Sabes, tengo mi lado romántico... vayamos a mi casa a ver cuánto tardas en descubrirlo."

P "Sabe, eu tenho um lado romântico... Vamos para minha casa ver quanto tempo você leva a descobri-lo."

S "Jag har faktiskt en romantisk sida...vi kan väl åka hem till mig och leta efter den?"

The Bar...

The Bar...

GB "Excuse me, you have some lipstick on your tooth. Do you mind if I lick it off?"

F « Excusez-moi mais vous avez du rouge à lèvres sur les dents. Puis-je vous l'enlever avec la langue ? »

D „Entschuldigung, Sie haben Lippenstift an den Zähnen. Kann ich ihn für Sie ablecken ? "

I "Mi scusi, ma ha un po' di rossetto sui denti. Le dispiace se glielo lecco?"

E "Perdona, tienes un diente manchado de pintalabios. ¿Te importa si te lo limpio de un lengüetazo?"

P "Desculpe-me, tem uma mancha de batôn nos dentes. Importa-se que a lamba?"

S "Ursäkta mig, men du har läppstift på din tand. Har du något emot att jag slickar bort det?"

The Bar...

GB "Forgive me if I'm trembling, but I'm terrified. I've never done this before. Can I buy you a drink?"

F « Pardonnez-moi si je tremble mais je suis terrifié. C'est la première fois que j'ose. Puis-je vous offrir un verre ? »

D „ Verzeihen Sie mir, wenn ich zittere, aber ich habe riesige Angst. Ich habe so etwas noch nie gemacht. Kann ich Ihnen einen ausgeben ? "

I "Mi perdoni se sto tremando, ma sono terrorizzato. Non l'ho mai fatto prima. Posso offrile da bere?"

E "Tendrás que perdonar este temblor, pero es que estoy muy nervioso porque es la primera vez que hago esto. ¿Te puedo invitar a una copa?"

P "Perdoe-me por estar a tremer, mas estou apavorado. Nunca fiz isto antes. Posso oferecer-lhe uma bebida?"

S "Ursäkta om jag skakar, men jag är livrädd. Jag har aldrig gjort det här förut. Får jag bjuda på en drink?"

The Bar...

GB "Girls say yes when they mean no, and no when they mean yes. Can I buy you a drink? Great!"

F « Les filles disent oui quand elles veulent dire non et non quand elles veulent dire oui. Puis-je vous offrir un verre ? Super ! »

D „Frauen sagen ja, wenn sie nein meinen, und nein, wenn sie ja sagen. Kann ich Ihnen einen ausgeben ? Großartig. "

I "Voi ragazze dite di sì, quando volete dire di no, e dite di no quando volete dire di sì. Posso offrirti da bere? Magnifico!"

E "Las chicas dicen que sí cuando quieren decir que no, y dicen no cuando quieren decir que sí. ¿Te puedo invitar a una copa? ¡Estupendo!"

P "As raparigfas dizem sim, quando querem dizer não, e não quando querem dizer sim. Posso oferecer-lhe uma bebida? Não? Óptimo."

S "Tjejer säger ja när de menar nej och nej när de menar ja. Får jag bjuda på en drink? Toppen! Vad vill du ha?"

The Bar...

GB "Here's 10p so you can call home and tell them you won't be home tonight?"

F «Voici 1 franc pour appeler chez vous et les prévenir que vous ne rentrerez pas ce soir.»

D „Hier sind 30 Pfennig, damit Sie Zuhause Bescheid sagen können, dass Sie heute nicht nach Hause kommen."

I "Eccoti £200 per chiamare i tuoi e dire loro che non torni a casa stanotte."

E "Toma cinco duros y llama a casa a decir que esta noche no vas."

P "Aqui tem uma moeda para telefonar e dizer que hoje à noite não vai."

S "Här har du två kronor så att du kan ringa hem och berätta att du inte kommer hem i natt."

The Bar...

GB "Hi! I'm Big Brother, and I've been watching you!"

F « Bonjour/Bonsoir! Je suis celui qui voit tout et je vous à l'œil depuis quelque temps! »

D „ Hallo ! Ich bin der große Bruder und beobachte Sie. "

I "Ciao! Sono la telecamera nascosta e ti sto osservando da un pezzo!"

E "¡Hola! Soy el Gran Hermano y te he estado observando."

P "Olá, eu sou o Big Brother, e tenho estado a vigiá-la."

S "Hej! Jag är Storebror och Storebror ser dig!"

The Bar...

GB "Hi, can I buy you several drinks?"

F «Bonjour/Bonsoir! Puis-je vous offrir plusieurs verres?»

D „Hallo, kann ich Ihnen mehrere ausgeben?"

I "Ciao, posso offrirti da bere molte volte?"

E "Hola ¿puedo invitarte a varias copas?"

P "Olá, posso oferecer-lhe várias bebidas?"

S "Hej, får jag bjuda på flera drinkar?"

The Bar...

GB "I suffer from amnesia. Do I come here often?"

F «Je suis amnésique. Je viens souvent ici?»

D „Ich leide an Amnesie. Bin ich oft hier?"

I "Soffro di amnesia. Sai se vengo spesso in questo bar?"

E "Sufro amnesia. ¿Vengo por aquí a menudo?"

P "Sofro de amnésia. Costumo vir aqui muitas vezes?"

S "Jag lider av minnesförlust. Brukar jag komma hit ofta?"

GB "I seem to have lost my phone number. Can I borrow yours?"

F « On dirait que j'ai perdu mon numéro de téléphone. Puis-je emprunter le vôtre ? »

D „Ich scheine meine Telefonnummer verloren zu haben. Können Sie mir Ihre leihen ? "

I "Credo di aver perso il mio numero di telefono. Mi presteresti il tuo?"

E "Me parece que he perdido mi número de teléfono. ¿Me prestas el tuyo?"

P "Parece-me que perdi o meu número de telefone. Pode emprestar-me o seu?"

S "Det verkar som om jag har tappat mitt telefonnummer. Kan jag låna ditt?"

The Bar...

GB "I would say that I'm in love with you, but you'd think I'm trying to pull a fast one."

F « Je vous dirais bien que je suis amoureux de vous mais vous penseriez que j'essaie de vous embobiner. »

D „Ich würde ja sagen, dass ich Sie liebe, aber Sie würden glauben, dass ich Sie abschleppen will."

I "Ti direi che mi sono innamorato di te, ma penseresti che sto cercando solamente di portarti a letto."

E "Podría decirte que estoy enamorado de ti, pero te pensarías que estoy intentando ligar contigo."

P "Eu diria que estou apaixonado por si, mas você poderia pensar que estou a tentar dar-lhe uma cantada."

S "Jag vågar inte säga att jag är kär i dig, då skulle du bara tro att jag försökte mig på ett snabbragg."

The Bar...

GB "I'm drunk."

F « Je suis saoul. »

D „ Ich bin betrunken. "

I "Sono ubriaco."

E "Estoy borracho."

P "Estou bêbado de êxtase."

S "Jag är full."

The Bar...

GB "I'm fighting the urge to make you the happiest woman on earth tonight."

F « J'essaie de me retenir de faire de vous ce soir la femme la plus heureuse sur terre. »

D „ Ich kämpfe gegen den Drang, Sie heute zur glücklichsten Frau der Welt zu machen. "

I "Sto combattendo il forte desiderio di renderti la donna più felice del mondo questa sera."

E "No sé como reprimir la necesidad de hacerte la mujer más feliz del mundo esta noche."

P Estou a lutar contra o impulso de fazer de si a mulher mais feliz do planeta esta noite.

S "Jag kämpar emot driften att göra dig till världens lyckligaste kvinna i kväll."

GB "I'm in the process of writing a telephone book. May I have your number?"

F « Je suis actuellement en train de rédiger un annuaire. Puis-je avoir votre numéro ? »

D „Ich schreibe ein Telefonbuch. Kann ich Ihre Nummer haben ? "

I "Sto cercando di scrivere una guida telefonica. Posso avere il tuo numero di telefono?"

E "Estoy escribiendo una guía telefónica. ¿Me das tu número?"

P "Estou a tentar elaborar uma lista telefónica. Dá-me o seu número?"

S "Jag håller på att skriva en telefonbok. Kan jag få ditt nummer?"

The Bar...

GB "Is it hot in here, or is it just you?"

F « Il fait chaud ici, ou est-ce simplement vous ? »

D „ Ist es sehr heiß hier, oder sind Sie das ? "

I "Fa caldo qui dentro o sei tu che me mi hai fatto alzare la temperatura?"

E "Hace calor aquí ¿no? ¿O eres tú?"

P "Está realmente quente aqui, ou é apenas você?"

S "Är det varmt här eller är det du som är het?"

The Bar...

GB "Lie down. I think I love you."

F «Allongez-vous. Je crois que je vous aime.»

D „Legen Sie sich bitte hin, ich liebe Sie."

I "Sdraiati. Penso di amarti."

E "Échate. Creo que te quiero."

P "Deite-se, penso que a amo."

S "Lägg dig ner. Jag tror att jag älskar dig."

The Bar...

GB "So, what do you do when you're not turning men to jelly?"

F «Alors, que faites-vous lorsque vous ne transformez pas les jambes des hommes en coton ? »

D „So, und was machen Sie, wenn Sie nicht gerade Männer in Wackelpudding verwandeln ? "

I "Allora raccontami che cosa fai quando non sei occupata a ridurre noi uomini in gelatina?"

E "Y así ¿a qué te dedicas aparte de dejar a los hombres como flanes?"

P "Então o que é que faz quando não está a transformar os homens em geleia?"

S "Vad sysslar du med när du inte får män att smälta?"

GB "So... How am I doing?"

F «Alors... Je me débrouille comment?»

D „So... wie komme ich zurecht?"

I "Allora... come sto andando?"

E "Bueno... ¿qué tal lo estoy haciendo?"

P "Então... Como me estou a sair?"

S "Du...hur går det för mig egentligen?"

The Bar...

GB "What is a slut like you doing in a classy joint like this?"

F « Qu'est-ce qu'une dévergondée comme vous fait dans un endroit aussi sélect ? »

D „Was hat eine Schlampe wie Sie in einem vornehmen Ort wie diesem zu suchen ? "

I "Che cosa ci fa una sciattona come te in un locale di classe come questo?"

E "¿Qué hace una golfa como tú en un sitio tan exclusivo como éste?"

P "O que é que uma ordinária como você faz numa espelunca de primeira como esta?"

S "Vad gör en slyna som du på ett sådant här elegant ställe?"

GB "Take your clothes off please, I want to compare the image in my mind with the real thing."

F « Déshabillez-vous s'il vous plaît, j'aimerais voir si l'image que je me fais de vous est proche de la réalité. »

D „Bitte ziehen Sie sich aus, ich möchte meine Vorstellung von Ihnen mit der Wirklichkeit vergleichen."

I "Spogliati per favore. Voglio fare il confronto tra l'immagine che ho di te nella mia mente e la realtà."

E "Quítate la ropa, por favor, quiero comparar la imagen en mi imaginación con la real."

P "Por favor, dispa-se. Quero comparar a imagem que tenho na cabeça com a imagem real."

S "Ta av dig dina kläder är du snäll, jag vill jämföra bilden i min fantasi med den äkta varan."

The Bar...

GB "Hi. You'll do."

F « Bonjour/bonsoir. Vous ferez l'affaire. »

D „Hallo, Sie würden mir genügen."

I "Ciao. Tu mi vai bene."

E "Hola. Me quedo contigo."

P "Olá. Você serve."

S "Hej. Du får duga."

The Bar...

GB "You aren't wearing make-up, are you? You look too good to tell for sure."

F « Vous ne portez pas de maquillage, n'est-ce pas ? Vous êtes si belle qu'il est difficile de se prononcer. »

D „ Sie tragen kein Make-up, oder ? Sie sehen zu gut aus, als das ich sicher sein kann. "

I "Non hai trucco, vero? Scusa, ma sei troppo perfetta per notare la differenza."

E "No llevas maquillaje ¿verdad? Estás demasiado guapa para decirlo con seguridad."

P "Não se maquilha, pois não? Você tem demasiado bom aspecto para se ter a certeza."

S "Du har inte sminkat dig, va? Du ser så bra ut att det är svårt att vara säker."

The Bar...

GB "You know, the woman I'd forget about for you is a blonde as well."

F « Vous savez, la femme que vous me feriez oublier est blonde elle aussi. »

D „Wissen Sie, die Frau, die ich für Sie zu vergessen versuche, ist auch blond."

I "Sai che la donna che ho completamente dimenticato per colpa tua è bionda anche lei?"

E "Sabes, la mujer que olvidaría por ti también es rubia."

P "Sabe, a mulher que eu esqueci por sua causa, também é loura."

S "Kvinnan jag skulle kunna dumpa för dig är blond hon också."

GB "You look confused. Drink I can you a buy?"

F «Vous avez l'air troublé. Offrir puis-je un verre vous ?»

D „Sie sehen verwirrt aus . Kann ich Ihnen einen ausgeben ?"

I "Mi sembri confusa. Offrirti bere posso da?"

E "Pareces confundida. ¿Invitarte a copa una puedo?"

P "Você parece desorientada. Bebida posso eu uma oferecer-lhe?"

S "Du ser förvirrad ut. Drink jag får en bjuda på?"

The Bar...

GB "You look like the type of girl who has heard every line in the book, so what does one more matter?"

F «Vous avez l'air de quelqu'un qui a déjà tout entendu, alors qu'est-ce qu'une tirade de plus?»

D „Sie sehen aus wie jemand, der alle Anmachen gehört hat, so was macht eine mehr schon aus?"

I "Mi sembri quel tipo di ragazza che ne ha sentite di tutti i colori, quindi cosa importa se senti anche la mia?"

E "Pareces el tipo de chica que ya ha oído todo tipo de cumplidos, ¿qué más da otro?"

P "Você parece o tipo de rapariga que já ouviu todo o tipo de propostas, por isso mais uma que diferença faz?"

S "Du ser ut som den sortens tjej som har hört alla raggningsrepliker så vad spelar en till för roll?"

The Bar...

GB "You must come here with those idiots to highlight your own beauty, right?"

F « Vous devez venir ici avec ces idiots pour mettre en valeur votre beauté, c'est ça ? »

D „ Sie sind mit diesen Idioten zusammen, um Ihre eigene Schönheit hervorzuheben, oder ? "

I "Mi sa che vieni qui con quelle svampite solo per far risaltare di più la tua bellezza, vero?"

E "Debes venir aquí con aquellos idiotas para que destaque tu propia belleza ¿verdad?"

P "Você tinha que vir aqui com todos aqueles idiotas, para fazer sobressair a sua beleza, não é verdade?"

S "Du går ut med de där nollorna för att framhäva din egen skönhet, eller hur?"

The Bar...

GB "You see my friend over there? He wants to know if you think I'm cute."

F « Vous voyez mon ami là-bas ? Il veut savoir si vous me trouvez mignon. »

D „ Sehen Sie meinen Freund da drüben ? Er will wissen, ob Sie mich niedlich finden ? "

I "Vedi quel mio amico laggiù? Vuole sapere se mi trovi carino."

E "¿Ves a mi amigo? Pues quiere saber si te parezco guapo."

P "Está a ver aquele meu amigo ali? Ele quer saber se você me acha giro."

S "Min kompis där borta vill veta om du tycker att jag är söt."

The Disco...

The Disco...

GB "Be unique. Step out from the crowd. Say yes."

F « Soyez unique. Démarquez-vous. Dites oui. »

D „ Seien Sie einzigartig. Unterscheiden Sie sich von der Masse. Sagen Sie „„ Ja"" "

I "Fai la diversa. Non fare la pecorona. Dimmi di sì."

E "Se único. Desmárcate. Di que sí."

P "Seja original. Saia da multidão. Diga sim."

S "Var unik. Skilj dig från mängden. Säg ja."

GB "Girls love me because I wear funky-coloured underwear."

F « Les filles m'adorent car je porte des sous-vêtements de couleurs très funky. »

D „Frauen lieben mich, schon wegen meiner bunten, witzigen Unterwäsche."

I "Le ragazze mi amano perchè i miei boxer sono rosso fuoco."

E "Las chicas me quieren porque llevo ropa interior de colores atrevidos."

P "As raparigas adoram-me porque visto roupa interior colorida."

S "Tjejer älskar mig för att jag har så häftiga underkläder."

The Disco...

GB "Congratulations! You've been voted Most Beautiful Lady in this Room and the grand prize is a night with me!"

F « Mes compliments! Vous avez été élue la Plus Belle Femme de ce Club et la récompense est une nuit avec moi! »

D „ Herzlichen Glückwunsch. Sie sind zur schönsten Frau im Raum gewählt worden, und eine Nacht mit mir ist der erste Preis. "

I "Congratulazioni! Sei stata votata La Donna Più Bella Della Sala e il primo premio è una notte con me!"

E "Felicidades. Has sido elegida la Mujer Más Bella De Esta Sala y el mejor premio es pasar una noche conmigo."

P "Parabéns! Você foi votada a Mulher Mais Linda Nesta Sala e o grande prémio é uma noite comigo."

S "Grattis! Du har valts till den vackraste kvinnan i detta rum och första priset är en natt med mig!"

GB "Do I know you from somewhere? I'm not sure I recognise you with your clothes on."

F « Je vous ais déjà vu quelque part, non ? Je ne suis pas sûr de vous reconnaître, comme ça, habillée. »

D „ Kenne ich Sie von irgendwoher ? Ich bin mir nicht sicher, ob ich Sie angezogen richtig erkenne. "

I "Ti ho già vista da qualche parte? Non sono sicuro di riconoscerti con i vestiti addosso."

E "¿Te conozco de algo? No estoy seguro de reconocerte con la ropa puesta."

P "Conheço-a de algum lado? Não tenho a certeza se a reconheço vestida."

S "Har inte vi setts förut? Jag är inte säker på att jag känner igen dig med kläderna på."

The Disco...

GB "I bet my girlfriend that I could pick up the most gorgeous woman here... So I guess I need your assistance."

F « J'ai parié avec ma petite amie que je pouvais dénicher la plus belle femme de cet endroit...J'ai donc besoin de votre aide. »

D „ Ich habe mit meiner Freundin gewettet, dass ich die schönste Frau in diesem Raum abschleppen kann...... ich glaube, ich brauche Ihre Hilfe dabei. "

I "Ho scommesso con la mia ragazza che stasera riuscirò ad abbordare la più bella donna qui dentro ... credo di aver bisogno della tua assistenza."

E "Me aposté con mi novia que podría llevarme a la tía más buena de aquí... Supongo que necesito tu ayuda."

P "Eu apostei com a minha namorada que podia conquistar a mulher mais elegante aqui presente... Por isso, suponho que preciso da sua assistência."

S "Jag slog vad med min flickvän om att jag skulle kunna ragga upp den läckraste kvinnan här...så jag antar att jag behöver din hjälp."

The Disco...

GB "Hi, I have been watching you dance for a while now, and to be honest, you are terrible, let me buy you a drink and we can talk about it."

F « Bonsoir, je vous regarde danser depuis un petit moment et, pour être franc, vous n'êtes pas terrible, laissez-moi vous offrir un verre et nous pourrons en discuter. »

D „ Hallo, ich habe Ihnen eine Weile beim Tanzen zugesehen, und um ganz ehrlich zu sein, Sie tanzen schrecklich schlecht. Ich gebe Ihnen einen aus und wir können darüber reden. "

I "Ciao, ti sto osservando da un po', e per dirti la verità, fai proprio pena come balli. Offrimi da bere e possiamo discuterne."

E "Hola. Llevo un rato mirando como bailas, y si he de serte sincero, eres malísima. Déjame invitarte a una copa y hablamos de ello."

P "Olá, há algum tempo que estou a reparar em si a dançar, e para ser honesto, você é espantosa, deixe-me oferecer-lhe uma bebida e podemos falar sobre isto."

S "Hej, jag har iakttagit dig på dansgolvet ett tag nu, och ärligt talat så dansar du uselt. Låt mig bjuda på en drink så kan vi tala om det."

The Disco...

GB "I don't love you, but I could!"

F «Je ne vous aime pas, mais je le pourrais!»

D „Ich liebe Sie zwar nicht, ich könnte mich aber dazu durchringen."

I "Non ti amo, ma potrei."

E "No te quiero, pero podría."

P "Não a amo, mas acho que podia."

S "Jag älskar inte dig, men jag skulle kunna!"

The Disco...

GB "1 love you. What's your name?"

F « Je vous aime. Quel est votre nom ? »

D „Ich liebe Sie. Wie heißen Sie ? "

I "Ti amo. Come ti chiami?"

E "Te quiero. ¿Cómo te llamas?"

P "Amo-a. Como se chama?"

S "Jag älskar dig. Vad heter du?"

The Disco...

GB "Make love to me, and I will die, or kill, as you command."

F « Faites-moi l'amour et je meurs, ou tue, selon votre désir. »

D „Kommen Sie mit mir ins Bett, oder ich sterbe oder töte, ganz wie Sie wünschen."

I "Fai l'amore con me e poi potrò morire, o uccidere, come tu comandi."

E "Hazme el amor y moriré o mataré según me ordenes."

P "Faz amor comigo, e a uma ordem tua, ou morrerei ou matarei."

S "Älska med mig och jag kommer att dö, eller döda, som du befaller."

The Disco...

GB "I'm not above begging!"

F « Je peux m'abaisser à implorer! »

D „ Ich bin mir nicht zu schade zum Betteln. "

I "Non trovo per niente degradante implorare!"

E "Si quieres te hago un favor."

P "Até sou capaz de implorar."

S "Jag kan till och med tigga om det om det skulle få dig att säga ja."

The Disco...

GB "Is that hair-colour natural? I'd like to check for myself."

F « Cette couler de cheveux est-elle naturelle ? J'aimerais le vérifier moi-même. »

D „ Ist die Haarfarbe echt ? Ich würde das gern selbst prüfen. "

I "Sono naturali i tuoi capelli? Mi piacerebbe controllare."

E "¿Es natural el color de tu pelo? Me gustaría comprobarlo yo mismo."

P "A cor do seu cabelo é natural? Gostaria de verificar por mim mesmo."

S "Är det din naturliga hårfärg? Jag skulle vilja se efter själv."

The Disco...

GB "My place or yours?"

F « Chez vous ou chez moi ? »

D „Meine Wohnung oder Ihre ? "

I "Da me o da te?"

E "¿Tu casa o la mía?"

P "Em minha casa ou na sua?"

S "Hem till dig eller hem till mig?"

The Disco...

GB "Say, that's a nice dress. Can I talk you out of it?"

F «Voilà une belle robe. Puis-je vous persuader de la quitter?»

D „Das ist aber ein schönes Kleid. Kann ich Sie zum Ausziehen überreden?"

I "Indossi un bel vestito. Posso convincerti a sfilarlo per me?"

E "Oye, qué vestido tan bonito. ¿Puedo convencerte de que te lo saques?"

P "É realmente um vestido bonito. Posso tirá-la daí de dentro?"

S "Det där var en snygg klänning. Har du något under?"

The Disco...

GB "You must be Greek, because you're a Goddess."

F «Vous devez être grecque, la plupart des déesses le sont.»

D „Sprechen Sie Griechisch? Wo Sie doch eine Gottheit sind?"

I "Devi essere greca perchè assomigli a una dea."

E "Debes ser griega, porque eres una diosa."

P "Você deve ser grega, porque é uma deusa."

S "Du måste vara grekiska. För du är väl en gudinna?"

The Disco...

GB "You smell. Want to take a shower together?"

F « Vous sentez un peu. Voulez-vous prendre une douche avec moi ? »

D „ Sie riechen nicht so gut. Sollen wir zusammen duschen ? "

I "Puzzi. Vuoi fare una doccia con me?"

E "Hueles. ¿Quieres que nos duchemos juntos?"

P "Você está com odor corporal... Tomamos banho juntos?"

S "Du luktar. Vill du duscha med mig?"

The Office...

The Office...

GB "'No Entry', right? Oh, just trying to guess your sign."

F « "Entrée interdite", pas vrai ? Oh, j'essaie juste de deviner votre signe. »

D „ „„ Nur für Personal "", oder ? Oh, ich versuche nur, Ihre Gedanken zu lesen. "

I "'Vietato l'ingresso', giusto? Oh, sto solo cercando di indovinare cosa c'è scritto sull'etichetta della tua gonna."

E "¿'Prohibida la entrada', correcto? Sólo intentaba adivinar tu signo."

P "'Proibida a Entrada', certo? Oh, estava apenas a tentar adivinhar o seu sinal."

S "Jungfru, eller hur? Va, nej jag försöker bara gissa ditt stjärntecken."

GB [At a copy machine] "Reproducing, eh? Let me help."

F [A la photocopieuse] « En train de reproduire, hein ? Je peux vous aider. »

D (An der Kopiermaschine) „ Reproduktion, eh ? Lassen Sie mich Ihnen helfen. "

I [Alla fotocopiatrice] "Riproduci, eh? Lascia che ti aiuti."

E [En una fotocopiadora] "¿Reproduciendo, eh? Déjame ayudarte."

P [Junto à fotocopiadora] "Reproduzindo, hein? Deixe-me ajudar."

S [Vid en kopieringsmaskin] "Jaså, du försöker reproducera? Låt mig hjälpa till."

The Office...

GB "Can you believe that just a few hours ago we'd never even been to bed together?"

F « Arrivez-vous à croire qu'il y a juste quelques heures, nous n'avions jamais couché ensemble ? »

D „ Kaum zu glauben, vor nur ein paar Stunden sind wir noch nie zusammen im Bett gewesen. "

I "Ci credi che fino a poche ore fa non eravamo mai stati a letto insieme?"

E "¿Puedes creerte que hace sólo unas horas ni siquiera nos habíamos acostado nunca juntos?"

P "Acredita que há apenas algumas horas nunca tínhamos ido para a cama juntos?"

S "Kan du tänka dig att för bara ett par timmar sedan hade vi inte ens gått till sängs med varandra?"

The Office...

GB "Do you know the difference between sex and watching a film? No? Great! Let's go to the cinema!"

F « Connaissez-vous la différence entre le sexe et regarder un film ? Non ? Super! Allons au cinéma ! »

D „Kennen ist den Unterschied zwischen Sex und einem Kinobesuch? Nein, – gut, lassen Sie uns ins Kino gehen. "

I "Sai che differenza c'è tra fare del sesso e guardare un film? No? Ottimo! Andiamo al cinema."

E "¿Sabes la diferencia entre el sexo y ver una película? ¿No? Qué bien ¡vámonos al cine!"

P "Sabe qual é a diferença entre sexo e ver um filme? ão? Óptimo! Vamos ao cinema."

S "Vet du vad skillnaden mellan att ha sex och att gå på bio är. Inte? Bra! Då går vi på bio!"

The Office...

GB "Hi, the voices in my head told me to come over here and talk to you."

F «Bonjour/Bonsoir, les voix dans ma tête m'ont dit de venir ici et de vous parler.»

D „Hallo, die Stimmen in meinem Kopf haben mir befohlen, herzukommen und mit Ihnen zu sprechen."

I "Ciao, le voci che sento nella mia testa mi hanno suggerito di venire qui a parlare con te."

E "Hola. Hay unas voces en mi cabeza que me dicen que venga aquí a hablar contigo."

P "Olá, vozes na minha cabeça disseram-me para vir aqui e falar consigo."

S "Hej, rösterna i mitt huvud sa till mig att gå hit och prata med dig."

GB "Hi. I'm the hand of God. Want a massage?"

F « Bonjour/bonsoir. Je suis la main de Dieu. Vous voulez un massage ? »

D „ Hallo, ich bin die Hand Gottes. Möchten Sie eine Massage ? "

I "Ciao, sono la mano di Dio. Vuoi un massaggio?"

E "Hola. Soy la mano de Dios. ¿Quieres un masaje?"

P "Olá. Sou a mão de Deus. Quer uma massagem?"

S "Hej, jag är guds hand. Vill du ha en massage?"

The Office...

GB "I may look like a nerd, but it's only a disguise."

F « Il se peut que j'ai l'air d'un crétin, mais c'est juste un déguisement. »

D „ Ich sehe vielleicht blöd aus, das ist aber nur eine Verkleidung. "

I "Posso sembrarti un cretino ma è solo un travestimento."

E "Debo parecer un borde, pero sólo es un disfraz."

P "Posso parecer um pateta, mas é apenas um disfarce..."

S "Jag kanske ser ut som en tönt, men det är bara en förklädnad."

The Office...

GB "I think you have the program to make my software into hardware."

F « Je pense que vous détenez le programme qui peut transformer mon disque souple en disque dur. »

D „ Ich glaube Sie haben das Programm, mit dem meine Software in Hardware umgewandelt werden kann. "

I "Credo che stai usando il metodo giusto per farmi diventare duro."

E "Creo que tienes el programa para poner mi ordenador a cien."

P "Penso que você tem o programa para transformar o meu software em hardware..."

S "Jag tror du har programmet som kan förvandla min mjukvara till hårdvara."

The Office...

GB "I'm doing a survey. Do you scream or moan?"

F « Je fais une enquête. Vous criez ou vous gémissez ? »

D „Ich mache eine Meinungsumfrage – schreien oder stöhnen Sie ? "

I "Sto facendo un sondaggio. Gemi o ansimi?"

E "Estoy haciendo un estudio. ¿Tú gritas o gimes?"

P "Estou a fazer uma pesquisa. Você grita ou geme?"

S "Jag håller på med en enkät. Skriker eller stönar du?"

The Office...

GB "Let's do breakfast tomorrow – should I call you or nudge you?"

F « Prenons le petit déjeuner demain – dois-je vous appeler ou vous donner un petit coup de coude ? »

D „ Lassen Sie uns morgen zusammen frühstücken – soll ich Sie anrufen oder Ihnen auf die Schulter tippen ? "

I "Facciamo colazione assieme domani mattina – devo chiamarti o devo darti una gomitata?"

E "Desayunemos juntos mañana. ¿Te llamo o te despierto de un codazo?"

P "Vamos tomar o pemqueno almoço juntos - quer que a acorde com um telefonema ou com uma cotovelada?"

S "Låt oss äta frukost i morgon – skall jag ringa och väcka dig eller bara knuffa till dig?"

The Office...

GB "My colleague and I made a bet, and I need to check if those are implants."

F « Mon collègue et moi avons fait un pari, et je dois vérifier s'il s'agit d'implants. »

D „ Mein Kollege und ich haben gewettet – jetzt muss ich prüfen ob das da Implantate sind. "

I "Io e il mio collega abbiamo fatto una scommessa e tocca a me controllare se quelle lì sono vere."

E "Mi amigo y yo hicimos una apuesta, y necesito saber si son implantes."

P "Os meus colegas e eu fizemos uma aposta, e eu preciso de verificar se elas são postiças."

S "Min kollega och jag slog vad och jag måste kolla om de där är av silikon."

The Office...

GB "My name is [your name], but you can call me at home tonight."

F « Je m'appelle [votre nom], mais vous pouvez m'appeler chez moi ce soir. »

D „Mein Name ist (Ihr Name), Sie können mich ruhig nach der Arbeit anrufen."

I "Mi chiamo [il tuo nome], ma tu mi puoi chiamare a casa stasera."

E "Me llamo [tu nombre], pero puedes llamarme en casa esta noche."

P "O meu nome é [o nome], e você pode telefonar-me para casa esta noite."

S "Jag heter [ditt namn], men du får kalla mig vad du vill när du ringer."

The Office...

GB "What's a great girl like you doing in an office like this?"

F « Qu'est-ce qu'une superbe femme comme vous fait dans un bureau comme celui-ci ? »

D „Was macht ein tolles Mädchen wie Sie in einem Büro wie diesem ? "

I "Che cosa ci fa un pezzo di ragazza come te in un ufficio come questo?"

E "¿Qué está haciendo una chica tan especial como tú en una oficina como ésta?"

P "O que faz uma garota formidável como você num escritório como este?"

S "Vad gör en fin tjej som du på ett kontor som det här?"

GB "You remind me of my first wife... Hot blooded, beautiful, and always furious with me!"

F «Vous me rappelez ma première femme... Passionnée, belle et toujours furieuse contre moi!»

D „Sie erinnern mich an meine erste Frau... heißblütig, schön und immer böse auf mich."

I "Mi ricordi la mia prima moglie ... ardente, bellissima e sempre furiosa con me!"

E "Me recuerdas a mi primera mujer. Sangre caliente, guapa y siempre furiosa conmigo."

P "Você lembra-me a minha primeira mulher... Sangue quente, linda e sempre furiosa comigo!"

S "Du påminner mig om min första fru....Varmblodig, vacker och alltid vansinnig på mig!"

The Office...

GB "You turn my system on."

F « Vous me mettez mon système sous tension. »

D „Sie machen mein System an."

I "Mi ecciti il mio sistema."

E "Has puesto en marcha mi sistema."

P "Você põe o meu sistema a funcionar."

S "Jag kan ett roligt dataspel: smeka musen."

Over the top...

Over the top...

GB "All those curves, and me with no brakes..."

F «Toutes ces sinuosités, et moi qui n'ai pas de frein...»

D „All diese Kurven und ich habe keine Bremsen..."

I "Tutte queste curve, e non ho nemmeno i freni ..."

E "Todas esas curvas, y yo sin frenos..."

P "Todas aqueles curvas e eu sem travões..."

S "Alla dessa kurvor och jag som inga bromsar har..."

Over the top...

GB "Are your legs tired? You've been running through my mind all day."

F « Vos jambes doivent être fatiguées ? Vous m'avez trotté dans la tête toute la journée ? »

D „ Sind Ihre Beine müde ? Sie sind den ganzen Tag durch meine Gedanken gelaufen. "

I "Hai le gambe stanche? È tutto il giorno che vai e vieni nella mia testa."

E "¿Tienes las piernas cansadas? Porque llevas todo el día circulando por mi mente."

P "Sente cansaço nas pernas? Você tem andado a correr durante todo o dia na minha cabeça."

S "Jag har suttit och funderat på något att säga till dig, men jag kom inte på något bra."

Over the top...

GB "Can I borrow some change? I want to call my mother and tell her I just met the girl of my dreams."

F « Puis-je vous emprunter de la monnaie ? Je voudrais appeler ma mère et lui annoncer que je viens de rencontrer la femme de mes rêves. »

D „ Können Sie mir etwas Kleingeld leihen ? Ich muss meine Mutter anrufen und ihr sagen dass ich meine Traumfrau getroffen habe. "

I "Puoi prestarmi della moneta? Voglio chiamare mia madre e dille che ho appena incontrato la ragazza dei miei sogni."

E "¿Tienes cambio? Quiero llamar a mi madre para decirle que acabo de conocer a la chica de mis sueños."

P "Pode emprestar-me alguns trocos? Quero telefornar à minha mãe e dizer-lhe que encontrei a mulher dos meus sonhos."

S "Kan jag få låna några kronor? Jag vill ringa min mamma och berätta att jag just träffat min drömtjej."

Over the top...

GB "Do you like short love affairs? I hate them. I've got all weekend."

F «Aimez-vous les histoires d'amour courtes? Je les hais. J'ai tout le week-end.»

D „Mögen Sie kurze Affären? Ich hasse sie. Ich habe das ganze Wochenende Zeit."

I "Ti piacciono le relazioni brevi? Io le odio. Ho tutto il fine settimana a disposizione."

E "¿Te van los rollos de una noche? Yo los odio. Tengo todo el fin de semana."

P "Gosta de namoros curtos? Eu detesto-os. Tenho o fim de semana todo."

S "Gillar du korta kärleksaffärer? Jag hatar dem. Jag har hela helgen på mig."

Over the top...

GB "Excuse me, but I think I dropped something under your chair – my jaw."

F « Excusez-moi mais je crois avoir laissé tomber quelque chose sous ma chaise – mes bras. »

D „Entschuldigung, ich glaube mir ist etwas unter Ihren Stuhl gefallen – mein Unterkiefer "

I "Mi scusi, ma credo di avere perso qualcosa sotto la sua sedia – la mia lingua."

E "Perdona, pero me parece que se me ha caído algo debajo de tu silla... la baba."

P "Desculpe, mas deixei cair uma coisa debaixo da sua cadeira – o meu queixo."

S "Ursäkta mig, men jag tror att jag tappade något när jag såg dig – min haka."

Over the top...

GB "Excuse me, but this is a non-smoking section and you happen to be on fire."

F « Excusez-moi mais il est interdit de fumer ici et je peux vous dire que vous faites un tabac. »

D „Entschuldigung, dies ist die Nichtraucherecke und Sie stehen in Flammen."

I "Mi scusi, ma questa zona è riservata ai non fumatori e lei è troppo focosa."

E "Perdona pero ésta es la sección no fumadores y tú estás que quemas."

P "Peço imensa desculpa, mas esta é uma área de não fumadores mas acontece que você está a arder."

S "Ursäkta mig, men det är rökfritt här och du är tänd."

Over the top...

GB "Screw me if I'm wrong, but isn't your name Rumpelstiltskin?"

F « Que je sois baisé si je me trompe, mais votre nom ne serait pas Rumplestiltskin par hasard ? »

D „Ich kann mich ja irren, aber heißen Sie nicht Rumpelstilzchen ?"

I "Che sia fottuto se non ti chiami Vattelapesca."

E "Jódeme si me equivoco pero ¿no te llamas Rumpelstiltskin?"

P "Chame-me doido se eu estiver enganado, mas você não se chama Rampelstiltskin?"

S " Fan ta mig om inte du är den elaka stymodern."

Over the top...

GB "Do you know what winks and screws like a tiger?" [Then wink]

F « Savez-vous ce qui cligne de l'œil et baise comme un tigre ? » [Puis, clignez de l'œil]

D „Wissen Sie, was blinzelt und wie ein Tiger im Bett ist ? " (Dann blinzeln)

I "Sai chi fa l'occhiolino e l'amore come una tigre?" [poi falle l'occhiolino]

E "¿Sabes qué guiña y jode como un tigre?" [Luego guiña un ojo]

P "Sabe o que pisca os olhos e faz amor como um tigre?" [Depois pisca os olhos]

S "Vet du vad som blinkar och knullar som en tiger?" [Blinka sedan]

Over the top...

GB "Let's go check out the shock absorbers in my new Ferrari."

F «Allons tester les amortisseurs de ma nouvelle Ferrari.»

D „Kommen Sie, lassen Sie uns die Stoßdämpfer in meinem neuen Ferrari ausprobieren."

I "Perchè non andiamo a provare gli ammortizzatori della mia nuova Ferrari?"

E "Vente a probar los amortiguadores de mi nuevo Ferrari."

P "Vamos testar os amortecedores do meu Ferrari."

S "Har du lust att testa stötdämparna i min nya Ferrari."

Over the top...

GB "You must be a top cheerleader... You've already got my spirit raised!"

F «Vous devez être la reine des majorettes... Vous avez déjà réussi à me remonter le moral!»

D „Sie müssen ein Top-Cheerleader sein... Sie haben meine Stimmung jetzt schon gehoben."

I "Saresti un giudice severissimo: con te pene sempre più duro."

E "Debes de ser una animadora estupenda... ¡Me has levantado la moral!"

P "Você deve ser uma animadora de primeira... Já me levantou a vitalidade!"

S "Du måste vara professionell cheerleader...Du har redan höjt stämningen!"

Over the top...

GB "I am an international spy. The safety of your country depends on you taking me to bed right now."

F « Je suis un espion international. Vous devez immédiatement me conduire à votre lit, la sécurité de votre pays en dépend. »

D „ Ich bin ein internationaler Spion. Die Sicherheit Ihres Landes hängt davon ab, dass Sie jetzt sofort mit mir ins Bett gehen. "

I "Sono una spia internazionale. La sicurezza del tuo paese dipende da te e da cosa sei disposta a fare a letto."

E "Soy un espía internacional. La seguridad de tu país depende de que te acuestes conmigo ahora mismo."

P "Sou um espião internacional. A segurança do seu país depende de você me levar para a cama imediatamente."

S "Jag är en internationell spion. Ditt lands säkerhet hänger på att du går till sängs med mig nu."

Over the top...

GB "I am very sexy, rich and extremely handsome... and what's your excuse for being so irresistible?"

F « Je suis très sexy, excessivement riche et extrêmement beau...quelle est votre excuse pour être si irrésistible ? »

D „Ich bin sehr sexy, reich und gutaussehend... und warum sind Sie so erotisch ? "

I "Sono un amante eccezionale, sono molto ricco ed estremamente bello ... qual è invece la tua scusa per essere così irresistibile?"

E "Soy muy sexy, rico e increíblemente guapo... y tú ¿qué excusa tienes para ser tan irresistible?"

P "Eu sou muito sexy, rico e extremamente elegante... e qual é a sua justificação para ser tão irresístivel?"

S "Jag är sexig, rik och oerhört vacker...och vad har du för ursäkt för din oemotståndlighet?"

Over the top...

GB "I don't think I've let money make me feel all that special."

F « Je ne pense pas avoir laissé mon argent me monter à la tête. »

D „Ich glaube nicht, dass mein Vermögen mich zu etwas Besonderen macht."

I "Non credo di essere tanto speciale solo perchè ho i soldi."

E "Creo que no he dejado que el dinero me haga sentir tan especial."

P "Não penso que tenha deixado o dinheiro fazer-me sentir tão especial."

S "Jag tycker inte att mina pengar gör mig så speciell."

Over the top...

GB "I'm a juggernaut of love, my brakes don't work and I'm headed straight for your heart."

F « Je suis un poids lourd d'amour, mes freins ne marchent pas et je me dirige tout droit vers votre cœur. »

D „ Ich bin eine Taube der Liebe, meine Bremsen sind kaputt und ich fliege direkt auf Ihr Herz zu. "

I "Sono un cannone carico di amore e le mie palle andranno dritte al tuo cuore."

E "Soy el tren del amor, voy sin frenos y de cabeza a tu corazón."

P "Sou um bólide do amor, os meus travões não trabalham e vou directo ao seu coração."

S "Jag är en bromslös långtradare lastad med kärlek på väg rakt in i ditt hjärta."

Over the top...

GB "I'm not drunk, you intoxicate me."

F «Je ne suis pas saoul, c'est vous qui me grisez.»

D „Ich bin nicht betrunken, Sie haben mich berauscht."

I "Non sono ubriaco, sei tu che mi fai girare la testa."

E "No es que esté borracho, es que me embriagas."

P "Não estou bêbado, você intoxica-me."

S "Jag är inte full, det är du som berusar mig."

Over the top...

GB "I've got the ship, you've got the harbour... let's tie up for the night."

F « J'ai le navire, vous avez le port... amarrons-nous pour la nuit. »

D „Ich habe das Schiff, Sie haben den Hafen.... lassen Sie uns für die Nacht festmachen."

I "Io ho la nave, tu hai il porto... perchè non ci ancoriamo per la notte?"

E "Yo tengo el barco, tu el puerto... atraquemos para la noche."

P "Eu tenho o barco, você o ancoradouro... Vamos atracar por esta noite."

S "Jag har skeppet, du har hamnen...skall vi lägga till för kvällen?"

Over the top...

GB "It's not the size that matters."

F « Ce n'est pas la taille qui compte. »

D "Non è la lunghezza quello che conta."

I „Größe spielt keine Rolle. "

E "Lo que importa no es el tamaño."

P "Não é o tamnho que importa."

S "Det är inte storleken som räknas."

Over the top...

GB "My love gun is loaded, and you are in my sights."

F « Mon canon d'amour est chargé et je vous ai dans ma mire. »

D „Mein Liebesgewehr ist geladen, und ich habe Sie im Visier."

I "La mia pistola dell'amore è carica, e tu sei nel mio mirino."

E "Llevo cargada mi pistola de amor, y te tengo en el punto de mira."

P "A minha arma do amor está carregada, e você está sob a minha mira."

S "Min kärlekspistol är laddad och jag har dig i siktet."

Over the top...

GB "Somebody call the police - it's got to be illegal to look that good."

F « Que quelqu'un appelle la police - il est impossible qu'une telle beauté soit légale. »

D „ Kann jemand die Polizei rufen - es muss illegal sein, so gut auszusehen . "

I "Qualcuno chiami la polizia - è sicuramente un crimine essere così belle!"

E "Que alguien llame a la policía... Tendría que ser ilegal ser tan guapa."

P "Alguém chame a polícia - tem que ser ilegal ter tão bom aspecto."

S "Ring polisen - det måste vara olagligt att vara så vacker."

Over the top...

GB "Was your father an alien? Because there's nothing else like you on earth!"

F « Votre père venait-il d'une autre planète ? Car il n'y a rien de comparable à vous sur cette terre. »

D „War Ihr Vater ein Außerirdischer ? So etwas wie Sie kann nicht von dieser Welt sein. "

I "Tuo padre era un extraterrestre per caso? Perchè non c'è nessuno come te su questo pianeta!"

E "¿Era extraterrestre tu padre? Porque no hay nada como tú en toda la tierra."

P "O seu pai era um extraterrstre? É que não há ninguém como você no planeta."

S "Var din pappa från yttre rymden? Det finns ju ingen som du i hela världen!"

Over the top...

GB "What time do you have to be back in heaven?"

F «A quelle heure devez-vous être de retour au paradis ? »

D „Wann müssen Sie wieder im Himmel sein ? "

I "A che ora devi rientrare in paradiso?"

E "¿A qué hora tienes que estar de vuelta en el cielo?"

P "A que horas é que você tem de regressar ao céu?"

S "Hur dags måste du vara tillbaka i himlen?"

Over the top...

GB "Would you be my love buffet? I'd like to lay you out on the table and take what I want."

F « Voulez-vous être mon buffet d'amour ? J'aimerais vous servir à table et prendre ce que je veux. »

D „Könnten Sie mein Liebesbuffet sein ? Ich möchte Sie auf den Tisch legen und mir nehmen was ich will. "

I "Vorrei che tu fossi la mia scatola di cioccolatini perchè così potrei aprirti e prendere quello che voglio."

E "¿Te gustaría ser mi bufé de amor? Te pondría sobre la mesa e iría picando lo que quisiera."

P "Você quer ser a minha refeição de amor? Gostaria de a pôr na mesa e tirar o que me apetecer."

S "Vill du vara min kärleksbuffé? Jag skulle vilja lägga upp dig på bordet och ta vad jag vill ha."

Over the top...

GB "You just think this is my leg."

F «Vous croyez sûrement qu'il s'agit de ma jambe.»

D „Sie müssen glauben, das hier sei mein Bein."

I "Immagina che sia la mia gamba."

E "Te crees que es mi pierna."

P "Você julga que é a minha perna."

S "Du bara tror att detta är mitt ben."

Over the top...

GB "You know, you look really hot. You must be the real reason for global warming."

F « Vous savez, vous faites brûler un tel désir autour de vous que vous devez certainement participer au réchauffement climatique. »

D „Wissen Sie, Sie sind wirklich heiß. Ich bin sicher das die Globale Erwärmung Ihre Schuld ist."

I "Lo sai che sei veramente piena di fuoco. Allora devi essere tu la causa del riscaldamento atmosferico!"

E "¿Sabes que pareces auténtico fuego? Debes ser la causa real del calentamiento global."

P "Sabe, você parece realmente quente. O aquecimento do globo dever ser por sua culpa."

S "Vet du vad, du ser riktigt het ut. Du måste vara det verkliga skälet till växthuseffekten."

Over the top...

GB "You're so sweet, you're going to put sugar out of business."

F «Vous êtes tellement à croquer que l'industrie alimentaire est en péril.»

D „Sie sind so süß, Sie werden den Zuckerhandel ruinieren."

I "Sei così dolce che non ho più bisogno di usare lo zucchero."

E "Eres tan dulce que vas a desbancar al sector del azúcar."

P "Você é tão doce, que vai pôr o açucar fora de circulação."

S "Du är så söt att sockerbolagen kommer att gå i konkurs."

Direct...

Direct...

GB "Are those 'screw me' eyes, or 'screw you' eyes?"

F « Ces yeux disent "baise-moi", ou "barre-toi" ? »

D „Sagen diese Augen „„Nimm mich"" oder „„Ich will Dich "" ? "

I "I tuoi occhi stanno cercando di dirmi qualcosa: è 'dammi piacere' o 'fammi il piacere'?"

E "¿Me estás mirando con ojos de 'jódeme' o de 'jódete'?"

P "Esse olhar quer dizer 'come-me' ou 'como-te'?"

S "Säger dina ögon 'ta mig' eller 'ta dig i brasan'?"

GB "Are you ready to go home yet?"

F «Alors, vous êtes prête à rentrer à la maison?»

D „Sind Sie jetzt fertig nach Hause zu gehen?"

I "Allora sei pronta per andare a casa?"

E "¿Estás lista para ir a casa?"

P "Já está pronta para ir para casa?"

S "Är det inte dags att vi går hem till dig?"

Direct...

GB "Excuse me, but would you like an orally stimulated orgasm?"

F « Excusez-moi mais désireriez-vous un orgasme stimulé par voie orale ? »

D „ Entschuldigung, kann meine Zunge Ihnen zum Orgasmus verhelfen ? "

I "Mi scusi, ma le piacerebbe avere un orgasmo orale?"

E "Perdona pero ¿te gustaría un orgasmo de estimulación oral?"

P "Desculpe-me, mas gostaria de ter um orgasmo oralmente estimulado?"

S "Ursäkta mig, men skulle du vilja ha en oralt framkallad orgasm?"

GB "Do you want to screw me or shall I apologize?"

F «Voulez-vous me baiser ou dois-je m'excuser?»

D „Wollen Sie mit mir ins Bett, oder soll ich mich entschuldigen?"

I "Vuoi che mi faccia fottere o mi devo scusare?"

E "¿Quieres joderme o tengo que pedir disculpas?"

P "Queres-me possuir ou devo pedir desculpa?"

S "Vill du knulla med mig eller skall jag be om ursäkt?"

Direct...

GB "Fancy coming back to my place for breakfast?"

F « Cela vous dirait de venir chez moi prendre le petit déjeuner ? »

D „Möchten Sie zu mir zum Frühstück kommen ? "

I "Hai voglia di fare colazione da me domani?"

E "¿Qué te parece ir a mi casa a desayunar?"

P "Gostarias de ir tomar o pequeno almoço a minha casa?

S "Har du lust att följa med hem till mig och äta frukost?"

Direct...

GB "I know you want me. You just don't know it yet."

F « Je sais que vous me désirez. Simplement, vous ne le savez pas encore. »

D „Ich weiß, dass Sie mich wollen. Sie haben es nur noch nicht gemerkt. "

I "So che mi vuoi. È che non lo sai ancora."

E "Sé que me deseas, sólo que tú aún no lo sabes."

P "Sei que me deseja. Só que você ainda não sabe."

S "Jag vet att du vill ha mig. Du vet bara inte om det än."

Direct...

GB "I bet you look great naked."

F « Je suis certain que vous devez être superbe nue. »

D „ Ich wette, Sie sehen nackt toll aus. "

I "Scommetto che sei fantastica nuda."

E "A qué estas imponente desnuda..."

P "Aposto que você fica bem toda nua."

S "Jag är säker på att du ser underbar ut naken."

Direct...

GB "1 love you. 1 want to marry you. Now let's screw."

F «Je vous aime. Je veux me marier avec vous. Bon, on peut baiser maintenant.»

D „Ich liebe Sie. Ich möchte Sie heiraten. Kommen Sie zu Bett."

I "Te quiero. Me quiero casar contigo."

E "Ti amo. Voglio sposarti. E adesso possiamo fare l'amore?"

P "Amo-te. Quero casar contigo. Vamos pôr, já."

S "Jag älskar dig. Jag vill gifta mig med dig. Nu när det är sagt så kan vi väl knulla?"

Direct...

GB "I think I'm falling in love with you. Can we go to bed yet?"

F « Je crois que je suis en train de tomber amoureux de vous. On peut aller au lit maintenant ? »

D „ Ich glaube, ich verliebe mich in Sie. Können wir jetzt ins Bett gehen?. "

I "Penso che mi sto innamorando di te. Possiamo andare a letto insieme adesso?"

E "Creo que me estoy enamorando de ti. ¿Ya nos podemos acostar?"

P "Creio que estou a apaixonar-me por si. Podemos ir para a cama?"

S "Jag tror jag håller på att bli kär i dig. Kan vi hoppa i säng än?"

Direct...

GB "I'm a very generous man, and I won't be happy until I've given you an orgasm."

F «Je suis un homme très généreux et je ne serais comblé que quand je vous aurai procuré un orgasme.»

D „Ich bin ein sehr großzügiger Mann und ich werde nicht glücklich sein, bis ich Ihnen zu einen Orgasmus verholfen habe."

I "Sono un uomo molto generoso e non sarò soddisfatto fino a quando ti darò un orgasmo."

E "Soy un hombre muy generoso y no me quedaré satisfecho hasta que te haya conseguido un orgasmo."

P "Sou um homem muito generoso, e não ficarei feliz enquanto não lhe provocar um orgasmo."

S "Jag är en väldigt generös man och jag nöjer mig inte förrän jag gett dig en orgasm."

Direct...

GB "I'll show you mine, if you'll show me yours."

F « Je vous montre le mien si vous me montrez la vôtre. »

D „ Ich zeige Ihnen meines, wenn Sie mir Ihres zeigen. "

I "Ti faccio vedere il mio, se mi fai vedere la tua."

E "Te enseñaré el mío si tú me enseñas el tuyo."

P "Eu mostro-lhe a minha, e você mostra-me a sua."

S "Jag visar min om du visar din."

Direct...

GB "I'm hung like a horse."

F « Je suis monté comme un cheval. »

D „ Ich bin wie ein Hengst gebaut. "

I "Sono dotato come un cavallo."

E "Estoy más colgado que un jamón."

P "Estou teso que nem um cavalo."

S "Jag är välutrustad som en hingst."

Direct...

GB "If it's sex you're looking for, just take me home now. No need to spend any more time here."

F « Si c'est de sexe dont vous avez envie, ramenez-moi à la maison tout de suite. Il n'est pas nécessaire de rester ici plus longtemps. »

D „Wenn Sie Sex suchen nehmen Sie mich einfach mit nach Hause. Es ist nicht nötig hier noch mehr Zeit zu verschwenden."

I "Se è sesso quello che vuoi, portami subito a casa tua. Non c'è motivo di sprecare altro tempo qua dentro."

E "Si lo que buscas es sexo, llévame a casa ahora mismo. No hay necesidad de pasar más tiempo aquí."

P "Se está à procura de sexo, leve-me já para casa. Não há necessidade de perder mais tempo aqui."

S "Om det är sex du är ute efter kan du ta med mig hem nu. Finns ingen anledning att ödsla mer tid här, eller hur?"

Direct...

GB "My face is leaving in 10 minutes... Be on it!"

F « Dans 10 minutes je mets les voiles... alors si vous voulez prendre ma barre!

D „Mein Gesicht geht in 10 Minuten... gehen Sie mit."

I "Il mio corpo se ne andrà tra 10 minuti. Vedi di esserci sopra."

E "Mi cara se marcha en 10 minutos... Márchate con ella."

P "As minhas rodas saiem dentro de de 10 minutos... Esteja nelas!"

S "Jag går om 10 minuter...skall du med eller?"

Direct...

GB "Pardon me, but may I attempt to seduce you?"

F « Pardonnez-moi mais puis-je tenter de vous séduire ? »

D „ Entschuldigung, kann ich versuchen, Sie zu verführen ? "

I "Mi scusi, ma potrei provare a sedurla?"

E "Perdona pero, ¿puedo intentar seducirte?"

P "Queira desculpar, mas posso tentar seduzi-la."

S "Ursäkta mig, men får jag försöka förföra dig?"

Direct...

GB "Should I call you in the morning, or nudge you?"

F « Dois-je vous appeler demain matin ou vous donner un petit coup de coude ? »

D „ Soll ich Sie morgen früh anrufen oder Ihnen einfach auf die Schulter tippen ? "

I "Per svegliarti domani mattina devo chiamarti o devo darti una gomitata?"

E "¿Te llamo por la mañana o te despierto de un codazo?"

P "Quer que a acorde de manhã com um telefonema, ou com uma cotovelada?"

S "Skall jag ringa och väcka dig i morgon eller bara knuffa till dig?"

Direct...

GB "That outfit would look great in a crumpled heap on my bedroom floor tomorrow morning."

F « Cette tenue serait superbe, toute froissée sur le sol de ma chambre demain matin. »

D „ Das Kleid sieht bestimmt großartig aus, wenn es morgen früh zusammengeknüllt auf dem Boden in meinem Schlafzimmer liegt. "

I "Il tuo vestito starà benissimo sul tappeto della mia camera da letto domani mattina."

E "Este traje quedaría muy bien hecho un lío en el suelo de mi habitación mañana por la mañana."

P "Essa roupa ficaria bem numa pila amorrotada no chão do meu quarto amanhã de manhã."

S "De där kläderna skulle se bra ut i en skrynklig hög på mitt sovrumsgolv i morgon."

Direct...

GB "Which is easier? Getting into that tight skirt or getting you out of it?"

F « Où réside la difficulté ? Rentrer dans cette jupe étroite ou vous en sortir ? »

D „Was ist einfacher ? Sich diesen engen Rock anzuziehen, oder ihn Ihnen auszuziehen ? "

I "Cosa è più facile? Entrarci in quella gonna o convincerti a togliertela?"

E "¿Qué es más fácil: meterse dentro de esta falda tan apretada o sacarte de ella?"

P "Qual das vias é mais fácil? Entrar nesse saia pequeníssima ou tirar-te de lá de dentro?"

S "Vilket är lättast? Att komma i den där tajta kjolen eller att få dig ur den?"

Direct...

GB "You have some nice jewellery. It would look great on my bedside table."

F «Vous portez de beaux bijoux. Ceux-ci seraient superbes sur ma table de chevet.»

D „Sie tragen wundervollen Schmuck. Der würde sich bestimmt gut auf meinem Nachtschrank machen."

I "Hai proprio dei bei gioielli. Starebbero veramente bene sul mio comodino."

E "Llevas una joyas preciosas. Quedarían fantásticas en mi mesita de noche."

P "Você tem jóias lindas... Que ficariam muito bem na minha mesinha de cabeceira."

S "Vilka vackra örhängen du har. De skulle passa väldigt bra på mitt nattduksbord."

Direct...

GB "You look like someone who should be kissed. Often. And by someone who really knows how."

F «Vous êtes une femme qui mérite d'être embrassée. Souvent. Et par quelqu'un qui sait vraiment comment.»

D „Sie sehen aus, als ob Sie geküßt werden sollten – und das oft – und von jemandem der wirklich was davon versteht."

I "Mi dai l'idea di qualcuna che ha bisogno di essere baciata. Spesso. E da qualcuno che sa quello che fa."

E "Deberías ser besada. A menudo. Y por alguien que realmente sepa cómo."

P "Você parece alguém que precisa de ser beijada. Frequentemente. E por quem realmente saiba como."

S "Du ser ut som någon som borde bli kysst. Ofta. Och av någon som verkligen kan sin sak."

Humorous...

Humorous...

GB "I expect that you're wondering why I have no nostrils."

F « Je suppose que vous vous demandez pourquoi je n'ai pas de narine. »

D „ Ich bin sicher, dass Sie sich fragen, warum ich keine Nasenlöcher habe. "

I "Ti starai chiedendo perchè non ho le narici."

E "Supongo que debes preguntarte por que no tengo nariz."

P "Espero que esteja admirada por eu não ter narinas."

S "Jag antar att du undrar varför jag inte har några näsborrar?"

Humorous...

GB "Bond. James Bond."

F « Bond. James Bond. »

D „ Bond. James Bond. "

I "Mi chiamo Bond. James Bond."

E "Bond. James Bond."

P "Bond. James Bond."

S "Bond. James Bond."

Humorous...

GB "Do you fancy coming back to my place for some sex and pizza? What, don't you like pizza?"

F « Cela vous dirait de venir chez moi pour un peu de sexe et de pizza ? Comment vous n'aimez pas la pizza ? »

D „ Haben Sie Lust, mit zu mir zu kommen, auf eine Pizza und etwas Sex ? Was , Sie mögen keine Pizza ? "

I "Vuoi venire da me per un po' di sesso e una pizza? Cosa? Non ti piace la pizza?"

E "¿Te apetece venir a mi casa, acostarnos juntos y comer una pizza? ¿Qué pasa, no te gusta la pizza?"

P "Gostaria de ir a minha casa para algum sexo e pizza? O quê, não gosta de pizza?"

S "Har du lust att följa med mig hem och ha sex och äta pizza? Va, gillar du inte pizza?"

Humorous...

GB "Do you know what a man with a huge penis has for breakfast? Well, I have bacon and eggs!"

F « Savez-vous ce qu'un homme doté d'un gros pénis mange au petit déjeuner ? Et bien, je prends des croissants! »

D „Wissen Sie was ein Mann mit einem riesigen Penis zum Frühstück ißt? Ich esse Spiegelei mit Schinken."

I "Vuoi sapere che cosa mangia a colazione l'uomo con un pene enorme? Beh, io prendo caffè e brioche."

E "¿Sabes lo que desayuna un hombre con el pene muy grande? Pues yo tomo huevos con bacon."

P "Sabe o que um homem com um grande pénis tem para o pequeno-almoço? Bem, eu tenho bacon e ovos."

S "Vet du vad en man med en enorm penis äter till frukost? Ja, jag kan ju bara tala för mig själv, och jag äter bacon och ägg!"

Humorous...

GB "I'm going to make love to you tonight whatever you say, so you might as well be there."

F « Je vais vous faire l'amour ce soir, quoi que vous disiez, alors ce serait aussi bien que vous soyez présente. »

D „ Ich werde heute Nacht mit Ihnen schlafen, was auch immer Sie sagen, so Sie können genauso gut dabei sein. "

I "Farò l'amore con te stanotte in una maniera o nell'altra, quindi tanto vale che tu sia presente."

E "Voy a acostarme contigo esta noche digas lo que digas, mejor que te presentes."

P "Hoje à noite vou fazer amor consigo diga você o que disser, por isso esteja lá também."

S "Jag tänker älska med dig i natt vad du än säger så du kan lika gärna vara med."

Humorous...

GB "Excuse me, can I borrow your bra?"

F « Excusez-moi mais puis-je vous emprunter votre soutien-gorge ? »

D „Entschuldigung, kann ich mir Ihren Büstenhalter leihen ? "

I "Mi scusi, posso prendere in prestito il suo reggiseno?"

E "Hola. ¿Me prestas tu sostén?"

P "Desculpe, pode emprestar-me o seu soutiã?"

S "Ursäkta mig, får jag låna din bh?"

Humorous...

GB "Excuse me, do you have sex with strangers? No. Well, then, allow me to introduce myself."

F « Excusez-moi mais couchez-vous avec les étrangers ? Non. Alors, permettez-moi de me présenter. »

D „ Entschuldigung, schlafen Sie mit Unbekannten ? Nein, erlauben Sie mir, mich vorzustellen. "

I "Mi scusi, ma è disposta a fare l'amore con gli estranei? No. Bene, allora permetta che mi presenti."

E "Perdona, ¿te acuestas con extraños? No. Bueno, entonces, permíteme que me presente."

P "Queira, desculpar. Costuma fazer amor com estranhos? Não? Então, permita que me apresente."

S "Ursäkta mig, brukar du ha sex med främlingar? Inte. Tillåt mig då att presentera mig."

Humorous...

GB "Screw me if I'm wrong, but don't you want to kiss me?"

F « Que je sois baisé si je me trompe, mais n'auriez-vous pas envie de m'embrasser par hasard ? »

D „Ich bin sicher das ich Recht habe, – Sie wollen mich doch küssen, oder ? "

I "Mandami pure al diavolo se ho torto, ma non vorresti baciarmi?"

E "Jódeme si me equivoco, pero ¿no quieres besarme?"

P "Sou todo seu se estiver enganado, mas não quererá você beijar-me?"

S "Jag kan ha fel, men du vill väl kyssa mig?"

Humorous...

GB Hey, little girl, how about a quick game of 'hide the weasel'?"

F « Eh, petite fille, et si on faisait une petite partie de "jambes en l'air" ? »

D „ Hallo, junge Frau, wie wär's mit einem schnellen Spiel Flaschendrehen ? "

I "Ehi, ragazzina, vuoi giocare con il mio trenino?"

E "Eh, monada, ¿jugamos a la comadreja y la madriguera?"

P "Ei, miúda, que tal um jogo rápido de "afagar o canário"?"

S "Hej, skall vi leka "gömma pitten"? "

Humorous...

GB   "Hi! Can I buy you a car?"

F   « Bonjour/Bonsoir, puis-je vous offrir une voiture ? »

D   „ Hallo, kann ich Ihnen ein Auto kaufen ? "

I   "Ciao! Posso comprarti una macchina?"

E   "Hola. ¿Puedo comprarte un coche?"

P   "Olá, posso oferecer-lhe um carro com duas rodas?"

S   "Hej! Får jag köpa dig en bil?"

Humorous...

GB "I need your help! I don't have a girlfriend by tomorrow, I'll lose my £10 million inheritance."

F « J'ai besoin de votre aide! Si je n'ai pas de petite amie d'ici demain, je perds mon héritage de 100 millions de francs. »

D „ Ich brauche Ihre Hilfe. Wenn ich bis morgen keine Freundin gefunden habe, verliere ich mein 10 Millionen Erbe. "

I "Ho bisogno del suo aiuto! Se non ho la ragazza entro domani, perdo un'eredità di 10 miliardi."

E "Necesito tu ayuda. Si mañana no tengo novia, perderé mi herencia de 2000 millones."

P "Preciso da sua ajuda! Se não arranjar uma namorada até amanhã, perco a minha herança de 10 milhões."

S "Jag behöver din hjälp! Om jag inte har en flickvän senast i morgon kommer jag att förlora mitt arv på hundra miljoner kronor."

Humorous...

GB "What does a guy like me have to do to get a phone number like yours?"

F « Qu'est-ce qu'un gars comme moi doit faire pour obtenir le numéro de téléphone de quelqu'un comme vous ? »

D „Was muss ein Mann wie ich machen, um eine Telefonnummer wie Ihre zu bekommen ? "

I "Che cosa deve fare un ragazzo come me per avere un numero di telefono come il tuo?"

E "¿Qué debe hacer un chico como yo para conseguir un número de teléfono como el tuyo?"

P "O que é que um tipo como eu tem que fazer para conseguir um número de telefone como o seu?"

S "Vad måste en kille som jag göra för att få ett telefonnummer som ditt?"

Humorous...

GB "Treat me right, and I can get you off Santa's naughty list!"

F « Si vous vous occupez bien de moi, je peux vous retirer de la liste noire du Père Noël. »

D „Wenn Sie nett zu mir sind, kann ich Sie aus dem schlechten Buch vom Weihnachtsmann entfernen lassen."

I "Se mi tratti bene potrei convincere Babbo Natale a toglierti dalla lista dei cattivi."

E "Trátame bien y te sacaré de la lista de niñas traviesas de Papá Noel."

P "Trate-me bem, e eu posso retirá-la da lista negra do Pai Natal."

S "Behandla mig schysst så skall jag se till att du inte blir svartlistad av tomten!"

Humorous...

GB "I can sense that you're a terrific lover, and it intimidates me a little."

F « Je devine en vous cette époustouflante amante et cela m'intimide un peu. »

D „ Ich spüre, dass Sie eine großartige Liebhaberin sind, und es macht mich ein wenig nervös. "

I "Posso capire che sei un'amante straordinaria e devo dire che questo mi intimidisce un poco."

E "Tengo la impresión de que eres una amante magnífica, y esto me intimida un poco."

P "Sinto que você é uma grande amante e isso intimida-me um pouco."

S "Jag känner på mig att du är en fantastisk älskarinna och det skrämmer mig lite."

Humorous...

GB "I think you would look great pregnant."

F « Je crois que vous seriez magnifique, enceinte. »

D „ Ich glaube, eine Schwangerschaft würde Ihnen großartig stehen "

I "Credo che saresti bellissima col pancione."

E "Creo que embarazada estarías guapísima."

P "Você ficaria magnífica grávida."

S "Jag tror att du skulle vara jättesnygg gravid."

Humorous...

GB "I think you're the most beautiful girl I've ever seen on a Wednesday."

F «Je pense que vous êtes la plus jolie fille que j'ai jamais vu un mercredi.»

D „Ich glaube, Sie sind die schönste Frau, die ich je an einem Mittwoch gesehen habe."

I "Credo che sei la ragazza più bella che abbia mai visto di mercoledì."

E "Creo que eres la chica más guapa que he visto en un miércoles."

P "Você é a rapariga mais bonita que vejo desde quarta-feira."

S "Du är den vackraste tjej jag någonsin sett på en onsdag."

Humorous...

GB "I'm a fertility god in some underdeveloped nations."

F « Je suis considéré comme un dieu de la fertilité dans certains pays sous-développés. »

D „ In einigen unterentwickelten Ländern gelte ich als Fruchtbarkeitsgott. "

I "Sono il dio della fertilità in uno dei paesi sottosviluppati."

E "Soy un dios de la fertilidad en algunos países subdesarrollados."

P "Sou um deus da fertilidade em algumas nações subdesenvolvidas."

S "Jag är en fruktbarhetsgud i ett underutvecklat land."

Humorous...

GB "I'm a magical entity! Take off your bra!"

F « J'ai un pouvoir magique! Retirez votre soutien-gorge! »

D „ Ich bin ein magischer Gott. Ziehen Sie Ihren Büstenhalter aus. "

I "Ho poteri magici! Togliti il reggiseno!"

E "Tengo poderes. ¡Sácate el sostén!"

P "Sou uma entidade mágica! Dispa o seu soutiã."

S "Jag är ett magiskt väsen! Ta av dig din bh!"

Humorous...

GB "I'm not wearing a bra, how about you?"

F «Je ne porte pas de soutien-gorge, et vous?»

D „Ich trage keinen Büstenhalter und Sie?"

I "Non porto il reggiseno, e tu?"

E "Yo no llevo sostén, ¿y tú?"

P "Não uso soutiã, e você?"

S "Jag har ingen bh, har du?"

Humorous...

GB "My girlfriend and I would like to experiment, and we both like you."

F « Ma petite amie et moi aimerions faire une expérience et vous nous plaisez à tous les deux. »

D „ Meine Freundin und ich möchten experimentieren und Sie gefallen uns beiden. "

I "Io e la mia ragazza vorremmo provare esperienze diverse e tu piacci a tutti e due."

E "A mi novia y a mí nos gustaría experimentar, y a los dos nos gustas."

P "Eu e a minha namorada gostaríamos de fazer uma experiência, e ambos gostamos de si."

S "Min flickvän och jag skulle vilja experimentera och vi gillar dig båda två."

Humorous...

GB "I only left home two days ago, and I don't know how to make the bed. I'm afraid we will just have to make love on the sofa."

F « Il n'y a que deux jours que je suis parti de chez mes parents et je ne sais pas faire mon lit. J'ai bien peur qu'il nous fasse faire l'amour sur le canapé. »

D „ Ich bin vor zwei Tagen Zuhause ausgezogen und ich kann mein Bett nicht machen. Ich fürchte, wir müssen unseren Sex auf dem Sofa haben. "

I "Sono andato a vivere da solo due giorni fa e non so ancora fare il letto. Mi dispiace ma dovremo fare l'amore sul divano."

E "Sólo hace dos días que salí de casa, y no sé como hacer la cama. Me parece que tendremos que hacerlo en el sófa."

P "Eu apenas saí de casa há dois dias, e não sei fazer a cama. Receio que tenhamos que fazer amor no sofá."

S "Jag flyttade hemifrån för bara två dagar sedan och jag vet inte hur man bäddar sängen. Vi får helt enkelt älska på soffan."

Humorous...

GB "Stand back, I'm a doctor. You go get an ambulance, I'll loosen her clothes."

F « Laissez-moi passer, je suis médecin. Allez chercher une ambulance, moi je vais dénouer un peu ses vêtements. »

D „ Machen Sie Platz, ich bin Arzt. Jemand anderes kann den Krankenwagen rufen und ich lockere ihre Kleidung . "

I "State indietro, sono un medico. Chiamate un'ambulanza, mentre io le tolgo i vestiti!"

E "¡Atrás, soy médico! Tú ves a llamar a una ambulancia. Yo le aflojaré la ropa."

P "Afastem-se sou médico. Vão chamar uma ambulância, eu tiro-lhe as roupas."

S "Skingra er, jag är läkare. Du hämtar en ambulans. Jag lossar på hennes kläder."

Humorous...

GB "Think of a number between 1 and 10. You lose – take all your clothes off!"

F « Choisissez un chiffre entre 1 et 10. Vous avez perdu – déshabillez-vous! »

D „Denken Sie an eine Zahl zwischen 1 und 10. Falsch... ziehen Sie alle Ihre Sachen aus. "

I "Pensa a un numero da 1 a 10. Hai perso – spogliati!"

E "Piensa un número entre el 1 y el 10. Has perdido, sácate la ropa."

P "Pense num número entre 1 e 10. Perdeu – dispa-se!"

S "Tänk på ett nummer mellan 1 och 10. Fel – ta av dig dina kläder!"

Humorous...

GB "Trust me. I'm a doctor. It might save your life."

F « Faites-moi confiance. Je suis médecin. Cela pourrait vous sauver la vie. »

D „Vertrauen Sie mir, ich bin Arzt. Ich könnte Ihr Leben retten. "

I "Non ti preoccupare, sono un medico. E potrei salvarti la vita."

E "Confía en mí. Soy médico. Puedo salvarte la vida."

P "Confie em mim. Sou médico. Posso salvar-lhe a vida."

S "Lita på mig. Jag är läkare. Jag skulle kunna rädda ditt liv."

Humorous...

GB "Want to see my stamp collection?"

F «Voulez-vous voir ma collection de timbres?»

D „Möchten Sie meine Briefmarkensammlung sehen?"

I "Vuoi vedere la mia collezione di farfalle?"

E "¿Quieres ver mi colección de sellos?"

P "Quer ver a minha colecção de selos?"

S "Vill du se min frimärkssamling?"

Humorous...

GB "Would you like to have a look at my war wounds?"

F «Voudriez-vous voir mes blessures de guerre?»

D „Möchten Sie meine Kriegsverletzung sehen?"

I "Vuoi vedere le mie ferite di guerra?"

E "¿Te gustaría ver mis heridas de guerra?"

P "Gostarias de ver as minhas cicatrizes de guerra?"

S "Skulle du vilja se mina ärr från kriget?"

Humorous...

GB "Why not come and party in my toolshed?"

F « Si on allait passer un bon moment dans ma cabane à outils ? »

D „Warum kommen Sie nicht mit und feiern mit mir in meinem Schuppen ? "

I "Vuoi venire a giocare con me nella mia soffitta?"

E "¿Por qué no vienes de juerga a mi cobertizo de herramientas?."

P "Porque não vem festejar no meu depósito de ferramentas?"

S "Vad sägs om att hänga med och festa i mitt redskapsskjul?"

Humorous...

GB "You're a lovelier sight than a beer truck pulling up in my driveway!"

F « Vous êtes plus belle qu'un livreur de vins se garant dans mon allée ? »

D „ Sie sind schöner als ein Bierwagen, der vor meinem Haus parkt. "

I "Averti è ancora più eccitante che possedere una cantina piena di vino pregiato!"

E "Me gustas más que un camión de cerveza parado a la entrada de mi casa."

P "Você é muito mais bonita do que um camião de cerveja a estacionar à minha porta."

S "Du är en vackrare syn än en långtradare med öl på min uppfart!"

Humorous...

GB "You've stolen my heart, but that's OK – I have three more back home in the closet."

F « Vous avez volé mon cœur, mais je m'en remettrais – j'en ai trois autres chez moi dans le placard. »

D „ Sie haben mein Herz gestohlen, aber das macht nichts – ich habe drei anderen Zuhause im Schrank. "

I "Mi hai rubato il cuore ma non importa – ne ho altri tre nell'armadio a casa."

E "Me has robado el corazón, pero no importa. Tengo otros en el armario de mi casa."

P "Você roubou o meu coração, mas está bem – tenho mais três em casa no armário."

S "Du har stulit mitt hjärta, men det är OK – jag har tre till hemma i garderoben."

Insulting...

Insulting...

GB "So, are those things real?"

F « Alors, ce sont des vrais ? »

D „ Sind die echt ? "

I "Dimmi, sono vere?"

E [Apuntando a los pechos.] "Oye ¿son de verdad?"

P "Estas coisaa são reais?"

S "Är de där äkta vara?"

Insulting...

GB "Are you free tonight, or will it cost me?"

F « Etes-vous libre ce soir, ou est-ce payant ? »

D „ Sind Sie heute Nacht frei oder muss ich dafür bezahlen ? "

I "Sei libera stasera o a pagamento?"

E "¿Estás libre esta noche o tengo que pagar?"

P "Estás livres esta noite, ou isto vai custar-me dinheiro?"

S "Är du ledig i kväll eller kostar det? "

Insulting...

GB "Can I buy you a drink or do you just want the money?"

F « Je peux vous offrir un verre ou voulez-vous juste l'argent ? »

D „Kann ich Ihnen einen ausgeben, oder wollen Sie nur das Geld ? "

I "Posso offrirti da bere o preferisci che ti dia i soldi?"

E "¿Puedo invitarte a una copa o sólo quieres el dinero?"

P "Posso oferecer-te uma bebida ou queres apenas o dinheiro?"

S "Får jag bjuda på en drink eller är du bara ute efter pengarna?"

Insulting...

GB "Didn't I have sex with your sister?"

F « N'aurais-je pas eu des rapports sexuels avec votre sœur ? »

D „ Habe ich nicht mit Ihrer Schwester geschlafen ? "

I "Sono andato a letto con tua sorella per caso?"

E "¿No me acosté con tu hermana?"

P "Não fiz amor com a tua irmã?"

S "Hade inte jag sex med din syster?"

Insulting...

GB "Hey, do you want to go halves on a bastard?"

F « Eh, ça vous dit de participer à la confection d'un bâtard ? »

D „ Hallo, wollen Sie einen Bastard mit mir machen ? "

I "Ehi, vuoi fare a metà con un bastardo?"

E "Oye ¿quieres hacer un bastardo a medias?"

P "Ei, quer ir a meias com um sacana?"

S "Du, vill du dela lika på en oäkting?"

Insulting...

GB "How did you achieve such a gaudy effect with cheap cosmetics?"

F «Comment avez-vous obtenu un effet si criard avec du maquillage si bon marché?»

D „Wie haben Sie nur einen solchen schlechten Effekt mit billiger Schminke erzielt?"

I "Come hai fatto a ottenere un effetto così pacchiano con quel trucco così vistoso?"

E "¿Cómo conseguiste este efecto tan llamativo con estos cosméticos tan baratos?"

P "Como é que consegues esse efeito pomposo com cosméticos baratos?"

S "Hur mycket billigt smink behövde du för att åstadkomma det här?"

Insulting...

GB "How much did you say your name was?"

F « Combien avez-vous dit vous appeler ? »

D „Wieviel haben Sie gesagt, kostet Ihr Name ? "

I "Quanto hai detto che costa il tuo nome?"

E "¿Cuánto has dicho que te llamas?"

P "Como é que disse que era o seu nome?"

S "Hur mycket sade du att du hette?"

Insulting...

GB "I love women who aren't afraid to put on a few pounds."

F « J'adore les femmes qui n'ont pas peur de prendre quelques kilos. »

D „Ich liebe Frauen, die keine Angst haben, ein paar Pfund zuzulegen. "

I "Amo le donne che non hanno paura di diventare grasse."

E "Me gustan las mujeres que no temen ponerse encima unos kilos."

P "Gosto de mulheres que não têm medo de gastar algum dinheiro."

S "Jag älskar kvinnor som inte är rädda för att gå upp ett par kilon."

Insulting...

GB "I've had quite a bit to drink and you're beginning to look pretty good."

F «J'ai pas mal bu et je peux dire que vous commencez à me plaire.»

D „Ich habe einiges schon getrunken, und langsam fangen Sie an, gut auszusehen."

I "Ho bevuto un bicchiere di troppo e cominci a sembrarmi carina."

E "Ya he bebido bastante y me estás empezando a parecer bastante potable."

P "Já bebi um bocado e começas-me a parecer bastante bonita."

S "Jag har druckit en hel del och du börjar se ganska bra ut."

Insulting...

GB "If I admitted you had an ugly body, would you hold it against me?"

F « Si j'admettais que vous n'avez vraiment pas un beau corps, vous m'en voudriez ? »

D „Wenn ich sagen würde, dass Sie eine schrecklich Figur haben, würden Sie das gegen mich verwenden ? "

I "Se ti dicessi che hai un corpo da fare schifo, lo useresti contro di me?"

E "Si te dijera que tienes un cuerpo muy feo, ¿lo apretujarías contra el mío?"

P "Se eu disser que tem um corpo feio, você atira-o contra mim?"

S "Du är fet och jag är full, men i morgon är jag nykter..."

Insulting...

GB "No, I'm not a policeman. What can I get for fifty pounds?"

F «Non, je ne suis pas de la police. Qu'est-ce que je peux avoir pour cinq cents francs?»

D „Nein, ich bin nicht von der Sitte. Was bieten Sie für fünfzig Mark?"

I "No, non sono un poliziotto. Cosa puoi offrimi con £100.000?"

E "No, no soy un policía. ¿Qué me haces por 4000 pesetas?"

P "Não, não sou polícia. O que posso obter por dez contos?"

S "Nej, jag är inte polis. Vad får jag för femhundra kronor?"

Insulting...

GB "You don't sweat much for a fat girl."

F «Vous ne transpirez pas beaucoup pour une grosse.»

D „Für ein dickes Mädchen schwitzen Sie wirklich nicht viel."

I "Non sudi tanto per essere così grassa."

E "Para lo gorda que estás no sudas demasiado."

P "Você não sua muito para uma rapariga gorda."

S "Du svettas ju inte så mycket för att vara så fet."

Insulting...

GB "You're prettier than my mum."

F «Vous êtes plus belle que ma mère.»

D „Sie sind doch etwas hübscher als meine Mutter."

I "Sei più carina di mia mamma."

E "Eres más guapa que mi madre."

P "Você mais bonita que a minha mãe."

S "Du är snyggare än min mamma."

Insulting...

GB "You're strangely sexy for such an ugly woman."

F «Vous êtes bizarrement sexy pour une femme si laide.»

D „Für eine häßliche Frau sind Sie überraschend sexy."

I "Sei incredibilmente provocante per essere così brutta."

E "Para lo fea que eres, resultas curiosamente sexy."

P "Você é extremamente bonita para uma mulher tão feia."

S "Du är ovanligt sexig för att vara så ful."

Insulting...

GB "Would you like to dance? I'm sorry, you must have misheard me. I said you look fat in that skirt."

F «Voudriez-vous danser? Je suis désolé, vous n'avez pas dû me comprendre. J'ai dit, cette jupe vous grossit.»

D „Möchten Sie tanzen? Tut mir leid, Sie haben mich falsch verstanden, ich habe gesagt, dieser Rock macht Sie dick."

I "Vuoi ballare? Oh, scusa ma credo che hai capito male. Ho detto che con quella gonna sembri più grassa."

E "¿Te gustaría bailar? Lo siento, me debes haber oído mal. He dicho que esta falda te hace muy gorda."

P "Gostaria de dançar? Desculpe, deve-me ter ouvido mal. Eu disse que você parecia gorda nessa saia."

S "Vill du dansa? Jag är ledsen, du måste ha hört fel. Jag sa att du ser fet ut i den där kjolen."

Romantic...

Romantic...

GB "Are you all right? It must be a long fall from Heaven."

F «Vous vous sentez bien ? C'est une longue chute, du paradis. »

D „Wie geht es Ihnen? Es muss ein langer Fall vom Himmel gewesen sein. "

I "Non ti sei fatta male, vero? Deve essere stata lunga la caduta dal cielo."

E "¿Estás bien? Debe haber sido una caída muy larga desde el cielo."

P "Sente-se bem? Deve ter sido uma grande queda do Paraíso."

S "Gick det bra? Det måste vara ett långt fall från himlen."

Romantic...

GB "As the sun illuminates the moon and stars, so let us illuminate each other."

F « Comme le soleil illumine la lune et les étoiles, brillons l'un pour l'autre. »

D „ So wie die Sonne den Mond und die Sterne zum Leuchten bringt, so könnten wir einander zum Glühen bringen. "

I "Così come il sole illumina la luna e le stelle, perchè non ci illuminiamo a vicenda?"

E "Como el sol ilumina la luna y las estrellas, iluminémonos el uno al otro."

P "Assim como o sol ilumina a lua e as estrelas, deixemo-nos iluminar um ao outro."

S "Såsom solen lyser upp månen och stjärnorna, låt oss lysa upp varandras skönhet."

Romantic...

GB "Can I have directions? To your heart."

F « Vous pouvez me dire le chemin ? Pour atteindre votre cœur. »

D „Können Sie mir die Richtung zeigen? Zu Ihrem Herzen . "

I "Mi puoi dare indicazioni? Per raggiungere il tuo cuore."

E "¿Me indicas el camino? A tu corazón."

P "Não se importa de me indicar o caminho? Para o seu coração?"

S "Kan jag få en vägbeskrivning? Till ditt hjärta."

Romantic...

GB "Do you have a map? I just got lost in your eyes."

F « Avez-vous une carte ? Je viens juste de me perdre dans vos yeux. »

D „ Haben Sie eine Landkarte, ich habe mich in Ihren Augen verirrt. "

I "Hai una cartina? Mi sono perso nei tuoi occhi."

E "¿Tienes un mapa? Acabo de perderme en tus ojos."

P "Tem um mapa? Acabo de me perder nos seus olhos."

S "Har du en karta? Jag gick just vilse i dina ögon."

Romantic...

GB "Don't worry about it. Nothing that's happened before counts. The only thing that matters now is that we're together."

F « Ne vous inquiétez pas. Rien de ce qui s'est passé auparavant ne compte. La seule chose importante maintenant, c'est que nous sommes ensemble. »

D „ Machen Sie sich keine Sorgen. Nichts von dem was bis jetzt passiert ist, war wichtig. Das einzig wichtige ist, dass wir jetzt zusammen sind. "

I "Non preoccuparti. Il tuo passato non conta per me. L'unica cosa importante è che adesso siamo insieme."

E "No te preocupes. No importa nada de lo que haya ocurrido antes. Lo único que importa ahora es que estamos juntos."

P "Não se preocupe com isso. Nada do que aconteceu antes conta. A única coisa que importa agora é que estamos juntos."

S "Oroa dig inte för det. Inget som hänt förr spelar någon roll. Det enda som betyder något nu är att vi är tillsammans."

Romantic...

GB "Excuse me, but do you have a life jacket? Because I'm drowning in your eyes!"

F « Excusez-moi mais avez-vous une bouée de sauvetage ? Car je suis en train de me noyer dans vos yeux. »

D „ Entschuldigung, haben Sie eine Schwimmweste ? Ich ertrinke in Ihren Augen. "

I "Mi scusi, ma ha un salvagente? Perchè sto affogando nei suoi occhi!"

E "¿Tienes un salvavidas? Me estoy ahogando en tus ojos."

P "Desculpe-me, tem um colete salva-vidas? É que estou a afogar-me nos seus olhos."

S "Du har möjligtvis ingen flytväst på dig? Jag håller nämligen på att drunkna i dina ögon!"

Romantic...

GB "Excuse me, do you mind if I stare at you for a minute? I want to remember your face for my dreams."

F « Pardonnez-moi mais, cela ne vous dérange pas si je vous contemple une minute ? Je veux me rappeler votre visage pour mes rêves. »

D „Entschuldigung, kann ich einige Minuten in Ihre Augen starren? Ich versuche mir Ihr Gesicht für meine Träume einzuprägen."

I "Le dispiace se la fisso per un attimo? Voglio ricordarmi il suo viso nei miei sogni."

E "Perdona ¿te importa que te mire un rato? Quiero recordar tu cara en mis sueños."

P "Desculpe, importa-se que olhe para si durante um minuto? Quero lembrar-me da sua cara nos meus sonhos."

S "Ursäkta mig, tar du illa upp om jag stirrar på dig en stund? Jag vill komma ihåh hur du ser ut när jag drömmer i kväll."

Romantic...

GB [Give her eleven roses] "Now you are holding them, it makes a dozen."

F [Offrez-lui onze roses] « Maintenant que vous les tenez, cela en fait douze. »

D (Geben Sie ihr elf Rosen) „Jetzt, wo Sie sie halten sind es zwölf."

I [Offrile undici rose] "Adesso che le hai in mano, la dozzina è completa."

E [Dale once rosas] "Ahora que las tienes tú, hay una docena."

P [Oferecendo-lhe onze rosas] "Agora que estão nas suas mãos, fazem doze."

S [Ge henne elva rosor] "Nu när du håller dem, blir det ett dussin."

Romantic...

GB "Hey, don't I know you? Yeah, you're the girl with the beautiful smile."

F « Eh, je vous connais non ? Oui, vous êtes la fille au si joli sourire. »

D „Hallo, wußten Sie es schon? Sie sind das Mädchen mit dem schönen Lächeln."

I "Ehi, non ci conosciamo? Sì, tu sei la ragazza con il bel sorriso."

E "Oye ¿no te conozco? Ah, eres la chica de la sonrisa bonita."

P "Ei, não a conheço de algum lado? Pois claro, você é a rapariga do sorriso bonito."

S "Känner inte vi varandra? Jo, du är tjejen med det vackra leendet."

Romantic...

GB "I don't know your name, but I'd really like to call you mine."

F « Je ne connais pas votre nom, mais j'aimerais beaucoup vous appeler du mien. »

D „Ich weiß Ihren Nachnamen nicht, aber ich möchte, dass Sie Meinen tragen."

I "Non so come ti chiami, ma vorrei tanto che fossi Mia."

E "No sé cómo te llamas, pero me gustaría llamarte mía."

P "Não sei o seu nome, mas gostaria de chamá-la minha."

S "Jag vet inte vad du heter, men jag skulle verkligen vilja kalla dig min."

Romantic...

GB "I found this rose and figured it had to belong to someone as beautiful as you."

F « J'ai trouvé cette rose et je me suis dit qu'elle devait appartenir à une femme aussi belle que vous. »

D „Ich habe diese Rose gefunden und habe mir gedacht, Sie gehört jemandem, so schön wie Sie"

I "Ho trovato questa rosa e ho pensato che dovesse appartenere a qualcuno bellissimo come te."

E "He encontrado esta rosa y he pensado que tenía que ser de alguien tan maravilloso como tú."

P "Encontrei esta rosa e achei que ela pertencia a alguém tão maravilhosa como você."

S "Jag hittade den här rosen och tänkte att den måste tillhöra någon som är så vacker som du."

Romantic...

GB "I must be lost. I thought paradise was further south."

F « J'ai dû me perdre. Je pensais que le paradis était plus au sud. »

D „ Ich muss mich verirrt haben, ich dachte, das Paradies war weiter südlich. "

I "Devo essermi perso. Pensavo che il paradiso fosse più a sud."

E "Debo estar perdido. Pensaba que el paraíso quedaba más al sur."

P "Devo estar perdido. Pensava que o paraíso ficava mais a sul."

S "Jag måste ha gått vilse. Jag trodde paradiset låg längre söderut."

Romantic...

GB "If I follow you home, will you keep me?"

F « Si je vous suis jusque chez vous, me garderez-vous ? »

D „Wenn ich Ihnen nach Hause nachlaufe, behalten Sie mich ? "

I "Se ti seguissi fino a casa, mi terresti per sempre?"

E "Si te sigo a casa ¿te quedarás conmigo?"

P "Se eu a seguir até sua casa, você toma conta de mim?"

S "Om jag följer dig hem, får jag sova över då?"

Romantic...

GB [Look at the label in her shirt] "I wanted to see if you were really made in Heaven."

F [Regardez l'étiquette dans son chemisier] « Je voulais voir si vous aviez vraiment été faite au paradis. »

D (Sehen Sie sich das Etikett in ihrer Bluse an) „Ich wollte nur sehen, ob sie wirklich im Himmel hergestellt wurde."

I [Leggi l'etichetta sulla sua camicetta] "Volevo vedere se sei veramente Made in Paradiso."

E [Mira la etiqueta de su camisa.] "Quería saber si estabas hecha en el cielo."

P [Olhando para a etiqueta na blusa] "Queria ver se você foi realmente feita no Paraíso."

S [Kolla på etiketten i hennes blus] "Jag ville bara se om du verkligen var gjord i himlen."

Romantic...

GB "Now I know why the sky has been grey all day... all the blue is in your eyes."

F « Désormais, je sais pourquoi le ciel est resté gris toute la journée... tout le bleu est dans vos yeux. »

D „Jetzt verstehe ich, warum der Himmel den ganzen Tag über so grau war, das ganze blau ist in Ihren Augen."

I "Adesso so perchè il cielo era così grigio oggi ... tutto l'azzurro è nei tuoi occhi."

E "Ahora sé porque el cielo ha estado gris todo el día...todo el azul está en tus ojos."

P "Agora sei porque razão o céu esteve cinzento durante todo o dia... o azul está todo nos seus olhos."

S "Nu vet jag varför himlen har varit grå hela dagen...allt det blå finns i dina ögon."

Romantic...

GB "Oh, they are shoulder blades. I thought they were wings."

F « Oh, ce sont bien des omoplates. Je pensais qu'il s'agissait d'ailes. »

D „Ah, das sind Schultern, ich dachte, es seien Flügel."

I "Oh sono le tue spalle, pensavo fossero ali."

E "Ah, son omoplatos. Creía que eran alas."

P "Ah, são chumaços para os ombros. Pensei que eram asas."

S "Jaså, är det skulderblad. Jag trodde det var vingar."

Romantic...

GB "So there you are! I've been looking all over for you – the girl of my dreams."

F « Alors, vous voici! Je vous ai cherché partout – la fille de mes rêves. »

D „ So, da sind Sie. Ich habe überall nach Ihnen gesucht – meine Traumfrau. "

I "Ecco, ti ho trovata! Ti ho cercata dappertutto – la ragazza dei miei sogni."

E "Así que estás aquí. He estado buscándote por todas partes. Eres la chica de mis sueños."

P "Finalmente a encontro! Tenho andado à sua procura por todo o lado - a rapariga dos meus sonhos."

S "Där är du ju! Jag har letat överallt efter dig – min drömtjej."

Romantic...

GB "There must be a rainbow nearby, because you're the treasure I've been searching for."

F « Il doit y avoir un arc-en-ciel quelque part, car vous êtes le trésor que je cherche depuis longtemps. »

D „Dies muss das Ende des Regenbogens sein, ich habe endlich den Schatz gefunden, nach dem ich gesucht habe."

I "Ci deve essere l'arcobaleno da qualche parte, perchè sei il tesoro che cercavo."

E "Debe haber un arco iris por aquí, porque tú eres el tesoro que he estado buscando."

P "Deve haver um arco-íris aqui perto, porque você é o tesouro de que eu ando à procura."

S "Det måste finnas en regnbåge i närheten, för du är skatten jag har letat efter."

Romantic...

GB "This is my pet rose. Would you please teach her how to be beautiful?"

F « Cette rose m'est chère. Voudriez-vous lui apprendre à être belle ? »

D „Dies ist meine Lieblingsrose. Könnten Sie ihr bitte beibringen, wie man so schön wird ? "

I "Questa è la mia rosa preferita. Le faresti vedere come si fa ad essere veramente belle?"

E "Esta rosa es mi mascota ¿podrías enseñarle cómo ser guapa?"

P "Esta é a minha rosa de estimação. Não se importa de lhe ensinar como ser maravilhosa?"

S "Detta är min leksaksros. Snälla, du kan väl lära henne hur man blir vacker?"

Romantic...

GB "Would you touch me please, so I can tell my friends I've been touched by an angel."

F « Voudriez-vous me toucher s'il vous plaît, pour que je puisse dire à mes amis qu'un ange m'a touché. »

D „ Könnten Sie mich bitte anfassen? Ich möchte meinen Freunden erzählen, dass ich von einem Engel berührt worden bin. "

I "Puoi toccarmi, per favore, così posso dire ai miei amici che sono stato toccato da un angelo."

E "¿Me tocas, por favor? Así podré decir a mis amigos que me ha tocado un ángel."

P " Não se importa de me tocar? Para que eu possa dizer aos meus amigos que fui tocado por um anjo."

S "Snälla, rör vid mig, så att jag kan berätta för mina vänner att jag blivit berörd av en ängel."

Romantic...

GB "You are the reason men fall in love."

F «Vous êtes la raison pour laquelle les hommes tombent amoureux. »

D „ Sie sind der Grund aus dem Männer sich verlieben. "

I "Sei la ragione per cui uomini come me perdono la testa."

E "Tú eres la razón por la que los hombres se enamoran."

P "Você é a razão por que os honens se apaixonam."

S "Du är anledningen till att män blir kära."

Romantic...

GB "You're so beautiful, I can't believe God didn't keep you for himself."

F « Vous êtes si belle, je ne peux comprendre que Dieu ne vous ai pas gardé pour lui-seul. »

D „ Sie sind so schön, ich verstehe nicht, warum Gott Sie nicht für sich selbst behalten hat. "

I "Sei così bella che non riesco a crederci che Dio non ti abbia tenuto per sè."

E "Eres tan guapa, que no entiendo por qué Dios no se te quedo para él."

P "Você é tão bonita, não posso acreditar que Deus não a tenha guardado para ele mesmo."

S "Du är så vacker att gud borde behållt dig för sig själv."

Romantic...

GB "You're what God had in mind when He said "Let there be woman"."

F « Vous êtes ce que Dieu avait à l'esprit quand Il créa la femme. »

D „Gott hat ganz bestimmt an Sie gedacht, als er sagte : " Es werde die Frau." "

I "Sei quello che Dio aveva in mente quando ha detto "e adesso creiamo la donna"."

E "Tú eres lo que Dios tenía en mente cuando creó a la mujer."

P "Você é o que Deus tinha em mente quando disse "Faça-se mulher"."

S "Du är vad gud tänkte på när han skapade kvinnan."

Romantic...

GB "Your daddy must be a thief. How else could he steal the sparkle of the stars and put it in your eyes?"

F « Votre père doit être un voleur. Sinon, comment aurait-il pu voler l'éclat des étoiles et le mettre dans vos yeux. »

D „ Ihr Vater muss ein Dieb sein. Wer sonst würde das Licht von den Sternen stehlen und in Ihre Augen tun ? "

I "Tuo papà deve essere un ladro unico nel suo genere. Come ha fatto se no a rubare lo scintillio delle stelle e a metterlo nei tuoi occhi?"

E "Tu padre debe ser un ladrón. ¿Cómo sino habría podido robar el brillo de las estrellas y ponerlo en tus ojos?"

P "O teu pai deve ser um ladrão. Porque roubou o brilho das estrelas e colocou-o nos teus olhos."

S "Din pappa måste vara tjuv. Hur skulle han annars kunna stjäla stjärnornas glitter och lägga det i dina ögon?"

Sexy...

Sexy...

GB "I want to taste your tan lines."

F « J'aimerais tester vos marques de bronzage. »

D „ Darf ich Ihre Bikinilinien ablecken ? "

I "Voglio assaggiare i segni della tua abbronzatura."

E "Quiero probar tus marcas del moreno."

P "Quero polir o teu bronze."

S "Jag bara måste se din bikinilinje."

Sexy...

GB "Your body is over 90% water, and I'm really thirsty."

F «Votre corps est constitué de 90 % d'eau, et j'ai vraiment soif.»

D „Ihr Körper besteht aus mehr als 90 % Wasser und ich habe großen Durst. "

I "90% del tuo corpo è acqua, e io ho tanta sete!"

E "Más del 90% de tu cuerpo es agua, y yo tengo una sed que me muero."

P "O teu corpo tem mais de 90% de água e estou cheio de sede."

S "Din kropp innehåller över 90% vatten och jag är väldigt törstig."

Sexy...

GB "Do you have a boyfriend? Would you like a spare?"

F « Avez-vous un petit ami ? Et un de rechange ? »

D „Haben Sie einen Freund? Brauchen Sie einen Ersatz, nur so für den Fall?"

I "Hai il ragazzo? Ne vuoi uno di scorta?"

E "¿Tienes novio? ¿Quieres uno de recambio?"

P "Você tem namorado? Gostaria de um sobressalente?"

S "Har du pojkvän? Vill du ha en reserv?"

Sexy...

GB "Erections like these don't grow on trees you know."

F « Des érections comme celle-ci ne poussent pas dans les choux vous savez.

D „ Errektionen wie diese wachsen nicht auf Bäumen. "

I "Erezioni come queste non crescono sugli alberi, sai?"

E "Erecciones como éstas no crecen en los árboles."

P "Erecções como esta não crescem nas árvores, sabe?"

S "Erektioner som denna växer inte på träd skall du veta."

Sexy...

GB "I'd like to get between your legs and eat my way to your heart."

F « J'aimerais passer entre vos jambes et vous dévorez jusqu'au cœur. »

D „Ich möchte zwischen Ihren Beinen sein und meinen Weg zu Ihrem Herzen schlemmen."

I "Vorrei farmi strada tra le tue gambe e a morsi raggiungere il tuo cuore."

E "Me gustaría meterme entre tus piernas y comerme el camino hasta tu corazón."

P "Gostaria de ficar entre as suas pernas e percorrer o caminho até ao seu coração."

S "Jag skulle vilja lägga mig mellan dina ben och äta mig upp till ditt hjärta."

Sexy...

GB "Hey baby, want to wrestle?"

F « Eh, chérie, si on faisait un peu de catch tous les deux. »

D „Hallo, Baby, wollen wir ringen?"

I "Ehi, bella, vuoi fare la lotta con me?"

E "Hola monada ¿quieres guerra?"

P "Oi minha, queres lutar?"

S "Hej snygging, vill du brottas?"

Sexy...

GB "Hi, my name is [your name]. Don't forget it, because you'll be screaming it later."

F « Bonjour/Bonsoir, je m'appelle [votre nom]. N'oubliez pas, car vous allez le hurler un peu plus tard. »

D „Hallo, mein Name ist... (Ihr Name). Bitte nicht vergessen, Sie werden ihn später rausschreien wollen. "

I "Ciao, mi chiamo [il tuo nome], e non dimenticartelo perchè è quello che fra poco griderai di piacere."

E "Hola, me llamo [tu nombre]. No lo olvides, porque lo vas a estar gritando más tarde."

P "Olá, o meu nome é [o nome]. Não esqueças, porque vais gritá-lo mais tarde."

S "Hej, Jag heter [ditt namn]. Glöm inte det för du kommer att skrika det senare."

Sexy...

GB "I don't bite... unless you ask me to."

F «Je ne mords pas...à moins que vous ne me le demandiez.»

D „Ich beiße nicht... es sei denn Sie bitten mich darum."

I "Non mordo ... a meno che tu lo desideri."

E "No muerdo... a menos que me lo pidas."

P "Eu não mordo... A menos que mo peças."

S "Jag bits inte...såvida du inte ber mig."

Sexy...

GB "I have a two-minute recovery time."

F «Je mets deux minutes à récupérer.»

D „Ich bin nach nur zwei Minuten wieder einsatzbereit."

I "Ho un tempo di recupero di due minuti."

E "Tengo un tiempo de recuperación de dos minutos."

P "Só preciso de dois minutos para recuperar."

S "Jag behöver bara två minuter för att återhämta mig."

Sexy...

GB "I know 101 uses for edible oil products."

F «Je connais 101 usages des produits huileux comestibles.»

D „Ich kenne 101 Anwendungsmöglichkeiten für Speiseöl. "

I "Conosco 101 modi diversi di usare prodotti commestibili a base di olio."

E "Conozco 101 usos para productos lubricantes comestibles."

P "Conheço 101 maneiras de usar produtos lubrificantes comestíveis."

S "Jag känner till 101 olika användningsområden för ätbara oljeprodukter."

Sexy...

GB "I need to take a shower. Do you want to come?"

F « J'ai besoin de prendre une douche. Vous voulez venir ? »

D „Ich muss duschen. Wollen Sie mitkommen ? "

I "Ho bisogno di una doccia. Vuoi venire?"

E "Necesito una ducha. ¿Te apuntas?"

P "Preciso de tomar um duche. Quer vir?"

S "Jag måste duscha. Vill du vara med?"

GB "I'd give you a piece of my mind, but I have more of something else."

F «Je vous donnerais bien mon avis, mais j'ai quelque chose de plus important à vous donner. »

D „ Ich würde Ihnen eine guten Rat geben, aber ich habe Besseres zu bieten. "

I "Ti potrei dare una mano, ma preferirei darti qualcosa d'altro."

E "Te diría lo que se me pasa por la cabeza, pero se me pasa más por otro sitio."

P "Dava-lhe um pedaço do meu espírito, mas tenho mais para lhe oferecer."

S "Jag borde ge dig en bit av mitt hjärta, men jag har mer av någonting annat."

Sexy...

GB "If I gave you sexy underwear, would there be anything in it for me?"

F « Si je vous offrais des sous-vêtements sexy, y aurait-il quelque chose pour moi dedans ? »

D „Wenn ich Ihnen sexy Unterwäsche schenken würde, wäre da was für mich drin ? "

I "Se ti regalassi della biancheria molto audace, me la mostreresti per vedere se la taglia è giusta?"

E "Si te regalara ropa interior sexy ¿habría dentro algo para mí?"

P "Se eu lhe der roupa interior sexy, poderei tirar de lá alguma coisa para mim?"

S "Om jag gav dig sexiga underkläder, skulle jag få ut någonting av det?"

Sexy...

GB "My name is [your name], but you can call me lover."

F « Je m'appelle [votre nom], mais vous pouvez m'appeler l'amant. »

D „Mein Name ist (Ihr Name), aber Sie können mich Liebling nennen."

I "Mi chiamo [il tuo nome] ma tu mi puoi chiamare amante."

E "Me llamo [tu nombre], pero puedes llamarme amante."

P "O meu nome é [o nome], mas você pode chamar-me amor."

S "Jag heter [ditt namn], men du kan kalla mig älskling."

Sexy...

GB "My tongue can do things for you that even drugs can't."

F « Ma langue peut vous donner des sensations que même des drogues ne peuvent vous donner. »

D „Meine Zunge kann Ihnen Freuden schenken, die nicht mal Drogen geben können "

I "La mia lingua potrebbe farti provare sensazioni che non riusciresti a provare nemmeno con la più potente delle droghe."

E "Mi lengua puede hacerte cosas que ni las drogas pueden."

P "A minha língua pode fazer por si coisas que nem mesmo as drogas conseguem."

S "Min tunga kan göra saker för dig som inte ens droger kan."

Sexy...

GB "Picture this: You, me, a bubble bath, a bottle of champagne..."

F « Imaginez : Vous, moi, un bain moussant, une bouteille de champagne... »

D „Stellen Sie sich das mal vor : Sie, ich, ein Schaumbad, eine Flasche Sekt... "

I "Immaginati noi due, una vasca piena di bolle di sapone, una bottiglia di champagne ..."

E "Imagínate esto: Tú, yo, un baño de burbujas, una botella de champaña..."

P "Imagine o seguinte. Você, eu, um banho de espuma, uma garrafa de champanhe..."

S "Föreställ dig det här: Du, jag, ett bubbelbad, en flaska champagne..."

Sexy...

GB "Sex is a killer. Want to die in my lap?"

F « Le sexe tue. Voulez-vous mourir sur mes genoux ? »

D „Sex ist ein Killer. Möchten Sie in meinem Schoß sterben ? "

I "Il sesso uccide. Vuoi morire tra le mie braccia?"

E "El sexo mata. ¿Quieres morir en mi regazo?"

P "O sexo é um assassino. Quer morrer no meu colo?"

S "Sex med mig är dödligt skönt. Vill du dö i mitt knä?"

GB "You have extremely good legs. What time do they open?"

F « Vos jambes sont très belles. A quelle heure ouvrent-elles ? »

D „ Sie haben tolle Beine, wann machen Sie sie auf? "

I "Hai delle gambe bellissime. A che ora si aprono?"

E "Tienes una piernas increíbles. ¿A qué hora abren?"

P "Você tem uma pernas divinas. A que horas é que elas abrem?"

S "Du har väldigt snygga ben. Hur dags öppnar dem?"

Sexy...

GB "Those would make great pillows!"

F « En voilà qui feraient de magnifiques oreillers! »

D „ Die würden tolle Kopfkissen abgeben. "

I "Sarebbero dei cuscini meravigliosi quelle due che hai davanti."

E "¡Qué delicia de almohadas!"

P "Que grandes almofadas elas fariam..."

S "De där skulle vara sköna som kuddar!"

Sexy...

GB "What nice legs you have. I'd enjoy wearing them as a belt."

F « Que vos jambes sont belles. J'aimerais tellement les porter en guise de ceinture. »

D "Che belle gambe che hai. Mi piacerebbe indossarle come cintura."

I „Was für tolle Beine Sie haben, ich würde die gern als Gürtel tragen. "

E "Que piernas más bonitas tienes. Me encantaría ponérmelas de cinturón."

P "Que belas são as suas pernas. Gostaria de usá-las como cinto."

S "Vilka fina ben du har. Jag skulle vilja ha dem som skärp."

Sexy...

GB "With one touch, I can have you making sounds which only dogs would hear."

F « D'un simple toucher, je peux vous forcer à émettre des sons que seuls les chiens pourraient entendre. »

D „ Mit einer einzigen Berührung kann ich Sie dazu bringen, Geräusche zu mache die nur Hunde hören können. "

I "Con il mio tocco, posso farti emettere suoni che solamente i cani sono capaci di sentire."

E "Con sólo tocarte una vez, te podría tener haciendo sonidos que sólo los perros consiguen oír."

P "Com um toque, posso levá-la a fazer sons que apenas os cães ouviriam."

S "Med en beröring kan jag få dig att utstöta ljud som bara hundar skulle höra."